ITALIAN CULTURAL STUDIES

•

2002

SELECTED ESSAYS

Edited by

Anthony Julian Tamburri

Library of Congress Cataloging-in-Publication Data

Italian Cultural Studies 2002 : selected essays / edited by Anthony
Julian Tamburri ... [et al.]
    p. cm. — (VIA Folios ; 36)
ISBN 1-884419-64-X
    1. Interdisciplinary Symposium of the Italian Cultural Studies
Association (4th : 2002 : Boca Raton, Florida).
    I. Tamburri, Anthony Julian. II. Title. III. Series: VIA Folios
(Lafayette, Ind.) ; 36.
HM623 .I555 2005
945.007 22   2005047113
                                                      CIP

© 2005, The Authors

Produced in the United States.

Published by
Bordighera Press
Languages & Linguistics
Florida Atlantic University
777 Glades Road
Boca Raton, FL 33431

VIA FOLIOS 36
ISBN 1-884419-64-X

TABLE OF CONTENTS

PREFACE

These essays represent a broad array of the papers delivered at the fourth annual conference of the Italian Cultural Studies Association.

It is also the fourth collection of essays available. The first collection was published by Bordighera Press in 2001, the inaugural publication of essays from the 1999 conference held at Dartmouth College; ICSA's second annual conference was held at Purdue University, in conjunction with the twelfth and last edition of the Purdue University Conference on Romance Languages, Literatures, and Film; the third and fourth conferences were held in Boca Raton, organized and generously sponsored by the Department of Languages & Linguistics and the Dorothy F. Schmidt College of Arts & Letters.

The essays in this collection originate from the two dozen papers delivered at the fourth annual ICSA conference that was held in conjunction with the international conference, *Global Diasporas and the United States: Exile, Migration, Race, and Ethnicity,* November 7-9, 2002.

Finally, I am most grateful to my co-organizers who offered much indispensable help in preparing for the conference.

Anthony Julian Tamburri
Florida Atlantic University
July 2005

Beyond Philology
Further Thoughts on Italian Cultural Studies

Anthony Julian Tamburri
FLORIDA ATLANTIC UNIVERSITY

In her keen introduction to the inaugural volume of this series, *Italian Cultural Studies*, Graziella Parati rightfully acknowledges the importance of philology to what we do today in this later realm of cultural studies.[1] This said, my preposition "beyond" does not possess exclusionary value; rather, it should be read as an indication of a point of origin. I would submit to the reader that philology, in all of it various manifestations, lies at the roots of what we do today in textual studies, those objects we understand as cultural productions be they written, visual, or aural.

Be it the end of modernism or the onslaught of the postmodern, the past few decades have constituted a period of transition, if not change, in the notion of globalization; and in intellectual circles today, many no longer tend to think in terms of an aesthetic hierarchy or the overly specialized. Instead, any national culture and its relationship with *other* internal and external cultural paradigms should now be taken into consideration and afforded greater significance as a topic of discussion.

By *other* internal paradigms, I have in mind gender, regionalism, and race, to name a few: by *other* external paradigms, instead, I have in mind not only different geo-political constructions – Spain, France, Germany, and the like – but also those paradigms we might readily consider *Italophone*. This said, then, one should not ignore the entire Italian diaspora that is both *internal* (e.g., Southern Italians heading north) or *external* (e.g., Italians going abroad for work, both in Europe and beyond).[2] In addition, we

---

[1] *Italian Cultural Studies*, eds., Graziella Parati and Ben Lawton (Lafayette, IN: Bordighera Press, 2001) viii.

[2] This sense of trans-european diasporistics has been adroitly discussed by Anna Camaiti Hostert in her *Passing: dissolvere le identità, superare le*

must also consider the more recent Italian phenomenon of immigration to Italy.[3]

It is therefore with regard to this new role, something that has already manifested itself in some intellectuals of *italianistica*, that the notions and tools of what we know as *cultural studies* and/or *multiculturalism* can significantly aid us. Indeed, the three significant works that come to mind thus far are *Italian Cultural Studies, An Introduction*; the special issue of *Annali d'Italianistica*; and *Italian Cultural Studies*.[4] These three collections represent, indeed, a developing trajectory of the notion of cultural studies within the more specific field we know as Italian Studies. Why it has taken so long for cultural studies to infiltrate Italian Studies has been aptly outlined by Dombroski:

> If we add these factors to the relative compactness and homogeneity of Italian society, that is to say, the lack of those circumstances which might have fostered the migration into Italy of non-Italian intellectuals and their entry into the academic disciplines and the public sphere, it is not hard to understand why the cultural studies phenomenon has been late in developing in Italy. By comparison, cultural studies in Britain and the United States, which was influenced to an important degree by the personal experiences of *emigrant intellectuals* from the Third World, was founded in part on the real experience of crossing cultural borders. (*Annali* 11-12; emphasis added)

This notion of "crossing cultural borders," both literal and metaphorical, has been keenly rehearsed in Parati's work

---

differenze (Rome: Castelvecchi, 1996), where she brings both an Italian and Italian/American perspective to the table.

[3] I refer my reader to the recent work of Graziella Parati on African/Italian writers, many of whom still write in their native language and are then translated into Italian. Equally important is Lucia Chiavola Birnbaum's study on black madonnas (*Black Madonnas: Feminism, Religion & Politics in Italy* [Northeastern University Press, 1993]), in which she employs a revisionist stance in examining this phenomenon from a multiculturalist point of view.

[4] *Italian Cultural Studies, An Introduction*, edited by David Forgacs (New York: Oxford UP, 1996); "Italian Cultural Studies" a special issue, edited by Robert Dombroski and Dino S. Cervigni, *Annali d'Italianistica* 16 (1998); *Italian Cultural Studies*, edited by Graziella Parati and Ben Lawton (Lafayette, Indiana: Bordighera Press, 2001).

on immigration to and migration within Italy.[5] Only when structures of power are interrogated together with and/or against a backdrop of notions of cultural aesthetics – i.e., the making of cultural productions within its specific socio-political *milieu* – can a methodology such as cultural studies come into play.

❖

In general, then, we may consider cultural studies as that mode of analysis that takes as its focal point of argument, as Stuart Hall tells us, "the changing ways of life of societies and groups and the networks of meanings that individuals and groups use to make sense of and to communicate with each other."[6] What is of primary significance is Hall's insistence on plurality – i.e., societies and groups – and interconnectedness – i.e., to communicate with each other. In this definition resonates indeed the original intent of *Italian Cultural Studies*, as Parati underscored in her introduction: "Expanding the field of specialization in order to explore new methodologies in defining a culture as a set of inter-twining strategies and of inter-relations" (ix).

In this spirit of expansion, cultural studies must then also be "critical" insofar as it must be more than the "mere description of cultural emergents that aims to give voice to the 'experience' of those who have been denied a space to talk," as Mas'ud Zavarzadeh and Donald Morton describe what they distinguish as "dominant" or "experiential cultural studies," which "offers a 'description' of the exotic 'other' and thus provides the bourgeois reader with the pleasure of contact with difference."[7] Instead, for them,

---

[5] One essay of hers I would refer to my reader is: "The Legal Side of Culture: Notes on Immigration, Laws, and Literature in Contemporary Italy," *Annali d'Italianistica* 16 (1998): 315-38. I would also point out several essays and anthologies by Armando Gnisci, specifically, *La letteratura italiana della migrazione* (Roma: Lilith, 1998), *Creoli, meticci, migranti, clandestini e ribelli* (Roma: Meltemi, 1998), *Una storia diversa* (Roma: Meltemi, 2001), and *Poetiche dei mondi* (Roma: Meltemi, 1999).
[6] See his essay, "Race, Culture, and Communications: Looking Backward and Forward at Cultural Studies," *Rethinking Marxism* 5.1 (1992): 10-18.
[7] See their co-authored study, *Theory, (Post)Modernity Opposition. An "Other" Introduction to Literary and Cultural Theory* (Washington, D.C.:

critical cultural studies "is not a description but an explanation, not a testimonial but an intervention: it does not
simply 'witness' cultural events, but takes a 'position' regarding them" (8). As both Hall and Zavarzadeh and Morton underscore, change is the operative word. For Zavarzadeh and Morton, especially, critical cultural studies
should constitute "an articulation of the cultural real that
will change the conditions which have blocked those
voices from talking" (8).

❖

Turning now to the premise that cultural studies represents, among other things as stated above, "the weakening of the traditional boundaries among the disciplines
and of the growth of forms of interdisciplinary research
that doesn't easily fit . . . within the confines of existing
divisions of knowledge" (Hall 11), we may then surely open
ourselves up to different modes of analysis that go beyond
those "traditional boundaries" of textual study so often
concerned with the formalistic, the historical, and the
thematic. Mere rhetoric and signification should not suf-
fice; other critical perspectives should become part of our
interpretive arsenal. This is especially true since many
contemporary Italian writers and visual artists today avail
themselves of certain generative tools that were not necessarily popular a decade or two ago, generative tools that
have their origin in a number of different sources – in
different national cultures, if not the *epistemological colli-
sion* of different national cultures;[8] in critical thinkers be-

---

Maisonneuve Press, 1991): 8. For Zavarzadeh and Morton, the propo-
nents of dominant cultural studies include the likes of John Fiske and
Constance Penley.

[8] I have in mind the case of the bicultural and bilingual writer. With specific regard to the Italian/American experience, see Paolo Valesio's
working paradigm in his substantive essay, "The Writer Between Two
Worlds: The Italian Writer in the United States," *Differentia* 3/4
(Spring/Autumn 1989): 259-276; and my review essay, "From *Simulazio-
ne di reato* to *Round Trip*: The Poetry of Luigi Fontanella," *Voices in Italian
Americana* 3:2 (1992): 125-134, which is an abbreviated version of my
later essay "Italian/American Writer or Italian Poet Abroad?: Luigi Fontanella's Poetic Voyage," *Canadian Journal of Italian Studies* Vol. XVIII,
No. 18 (1995): 76-92.

coming creative writers; in the influence of other media on the written word; in the incorporation of popular cultural forms with those considered more high-brow; in the *high-browization* and/or glorification of the popular arts – e.g., film, romance narratives, and music videos; or, finally, the fact that Italy now finds itself with an immigrant generation it has never seen before.

One such arsenal we may wish to investigate as a source of critical ammunition is that dedicated to the examination of post-colonial literature. A young Aijaz Ahmad had proposed some intriguing thoughts in the late 1980s that, I would suggest, remain equally relevant. First, that any cultural product, to generalize for our purposes here, cannot be "constructed as an internally coherent object of theoretical knowledge"; that such a categorization "cannot be resolved . . . without an altogether positivist reductionism."[9] Secondly, *other* "[aesthetic] traditions [e.g., third world, ethnic, etc.] remain, beyond a few texts here and there, [often] unknown to the [...] theorist" (5) not familiar with the local terrain. Thirdly, and perhaps most relevant, "[aesthetic] texts are produced in highly differentiated, usually over-determined contexts of *competing ideological and cultural clusters, so that any particular text of any complexity shall always have to be placed within the cluster that gives it its energy and form, before it is totalised into a universal category*" (23; my emphasis). These three notions, I would submit, constitute a significant ideological framework of cluster specificity within which Italian intellectuals could, and indeed should, consider further the notion of, for example, regional literature *qua* Italian literature and re-think the significance of the Italian writer and/or visual artist within such re-categorization of the notion of the so-called *regional writer*.

Because of the work of some critics who have offered alternative perspectives through some of the more recent analytical and interpretive tools of hermeneutics, deconstruction, semiotics, and the like, we can readily broaden

---

[9]See Aijaz Ahmad's response: "Jameson's Rhetoric of Otherness and the 'National Allegory'," *Social Text* 17 (1987): 4; now in *In Theory* (London: Verso, 1992).

our view of what constitutes the Italian experience in the arts. I would thus propose that we reconsider *italianistica*, for instance, to be a series of on-going aesthetic enterprises that establish a repertoire of signs, at times, *sui generis*, and therefore create variations (verbal and/or visual, in the case of film, painting, sculpture, drama, etc.) that represent different versions – dependent, of course, on one's generation, gender, socio-economic condition – of what can be perceived as the Italian *interpretant*.[10] That is, the Italian experience may indeed be manifested in any art form in a number of ways and at varying degrees, for which one may readily speak of the variegated representations of the Italian ethos in literature, for example, in the same fashion in which Daniel Aaron spoke of the "hyphenate writer"[11] and Aijaz Ahmad discussed new ways of considering "third-world" literature.

❖

Concerning the notion of cultural studies and its validity and significance to Italy, we might list some suggestions with regard to the construction and maintenance of an Italian cultural studies discourse. First and foremost, Italian intellectuals must define their terms. In this great-

---

[10]I have opted for the Peircean categories of *sign* (or *representamen*) and *interpretant*, as opposed to the Saussarean couplet of signifier/signified for distinguishing between the image and the concept. Peirce's defintion of the sign is: "A sign or *representamen*, is something which stands for something in some respect or capacity. It addresses somebody, that is creates in the mind of that person an equivalent sign, or perhaps a more developed sign. The sign which it creates I call the *interpretant* of the first sign. The sign stands for something, its *object*. It stands for that object, not in all respects, but in reference to a sort of idea, which I have sometimes called the *ground* of the representamen" (2.228; emphasis textual). See his *Principles of Philosophy* in *Collected Papers*, eds., Charles Hartshorne and Paul Weiss (Cambridge, MA: Harvard UP, 1960). For more on the difference between Peircean and Saussurean notions of the sign, see Floyd Merrell's recent study, *Sign, Textuality, World* (Bloomington: Indiana UP, 1992): 3-73 especially.

[11]See, "The Hyphenate Writer and American Letters," *Smith Alumnae Quarterly* (July 1964): 213-7; later revised in *Rivista di Studi Anglo-Americani* 3.4-5 (1984-85): 11-28, and Anthony Julian Tamburri, *To Hyphenate or Not to Hyphenate: The Italian/American Writer: An Other American* (Montreal: Guernica Editions, 1991).

er growing semantic web of multiple discourses, we cannot continue to conflate terminology. Namely, as a "theory (albeit vague) about the *foundations* of a culture rather than a practice which subsumes cultural ideas,"[12] and within the greater discourse of a greater Italy and all of its regions – and here let us extend our notion of region beyond the geo-political borders of Italy–, multiculturalism figures as a general phenomenon with all of Italy as the historical intertext for a better understanding of the Italian phenomenon.[13]

Secondly, one must cross borders today geo-intellectually, as James Clifford signaled as far back as two decades ago: "Cultural analysis is always enmeshed in global movements of difference and power. However one defines it, and the phrase is here used loosely, a 'world system' now links the planet's societies in a common historical process" (22).[14] Programs of an interdisciplinary nature, for instance, should be set up to include courses from an array of departments and/or programs – e.g., Italian, Sociology, History, Political Science, English – that would readily form an undergraduate major that could easily be integrated into a double major. A similar program is also readily feasible on the graduate level. Programs/departments of Comparative Literature or Comparative Studies – as well as more recent Cultural Studies Programs – can be fertile ground for this type of program. This, in fact, is the set-up at Florida Atlantic University, where graduate students working for the Ph.D. in Comparative Studies have the option of Multicultural U.S. Literature, Italian/American studies, or any other such designation of a similarly

---

[12] Martin Harrison, "On a Poem of Gun Gencer's," in *Multicultural Australia*, eds. J. Delaruelle and Karakostas-Seda (Sidney: Australia Council for the Literature Board, 1985): 128.

[13] Indeed, for the construction of any cultural studies discourse, historical specificity is of prime importance, as even Hall reminds us (12). Such specificity of each cultural configuration and pattern, then, can be examined with these new analytical and interpretive tools for an eventual reconciliation of the specific group in question with those of the other groups that constitute the greater poli-cultural mosaic of the United States.

[14] See his "Introduction," *Writing Culture: The Poetics and Politics of Ethnography* (Berkeley: U California P, 1986).

diverse nature, as either of their two areas of study; and where courses on such subject matter are regularly cross-listed with other disciplines, for which globalization of this sort must be poly-cultural.[15]

Such strategies and calls to action respond to a necessity of inclusiveness of all groups. For until all groups – the so-called dominant class *and* non-dominants – are included in a cultural discourse, we run the risk of: 1) maintaining the obvious aesthetic hierarchy of a major art forms and numerous minor art forms; and 2) conserving the divisiveness that seems to exist today, precisely because an aesthetic hierarchy is maintained, both within and outside of the community of *italianistica* of, for example, creative writers and critical thinkers. With "its focus on the politics of the production of subjectivities rather than on textual operations, [cultural studies] understands 'politics' as access to the material base of [power, knowledge, and resources]" (Zavarzadeh and Morton 208). Cultural studies also "insists on the necessity to address [these] central, urgent, and disturbing questions of a society and a culture [in] the most rigorous intellectual way . . . available" (Hall 11). It thus constitutes, as he continues, "one of the points of tension and change at the frontiers of intellectual and academic life, pushing for new questions, new models, and new ways of study, testing the fine lines between intellectual rigor and social relevance" (11). For only when all these concerns are addressed and all identifiable Italian (read also, Italophone) groups and their differences are foregrounded on equal terms through an exploratory lens such as that of cultural studies – one thing that must take place both within and outside the Italian community – only then can the notion of multiculturalism function effectively as a useful expression of difference,[16] and cultural studies as a useful tool of investi-

---

[15] Indeed, as Irene Kacandes states, "we need to make the case most strongly to our students and our administrations that this is not the time to be monocultural or monolingual" ("What Is at Stake in Doing Cultural Studies," *Italian Cultural Studies*, 9).

[16] For an excellent example of this notion put into effect, see Sneja Gunew, "Denaturalizing Cultural Nationalisms: Multicultural Readings of

gation, leading ultimately to a more level field of play for critical discourse and intellectual exchange.

'Australia'" in *Nation and Narration*, ed. Homi K. Bhabha (London: Routledge, 1990): 99-112.

Refiguring History through the Exotic: Gianni Celati's *bazar archeologico* and Toni Maraini's *mosaico d'oriente*

Cinzia Sartini Blum
THE UNIVERSITY OF IOWA

"[N]elle figure di finzione l'importanza sta nella peripezia attraverso cui ci portano, la danza a cui ci persuadono, i movimenti a cui ci conducono [. . .]. E allora la peripezia di esposizione del discorso archeologico si offre come il tracciato di un diverso itinerario, diverso rispetto all'utopia, che è la figura spaziale dell'agnizione storica: [. . .] una *quête* senza meta, spazializzazione e *flânerie*, ininterrotta visita ai luoghi molecolari d'una città eterotopica dove galleggiano all'infinito residui di estraneità, oggetti e tracce di ciò che si è perduto e nessun museo è disposto a conservare." (Celati, "Il bazar archeologico" 207)

"[L]a storia è una catena dai tanti anelli diramanti ricollegati ad altre catene che attraversano il tempo con invidiabile affascinante disinvoltura e farla morire è arduo; anche se già si dissolve nel continuo presente del brodo mediatico. Per chi come noi si ostina ad amarla e interrogarla, tutto è ricollegato in una trama di tasselli e fili trascinati dal tempo. Eterno ritorno o fiume pitagorico che sia, fluisce costante e lascia segni. Finita o non finita, questa epopea di memorie ci aiuta ad affrontare oggi il frullato omogeneizzato dei segni. Alla loro ricerca, i nostri spostamenti sono avvenuti nello spazio e nel tempo." (Maraini, *Ultimo Tè a Marrakesh* 15)

W estern intellectual history can be scribed as a progression of totalizing systems of thought, built on theological and philosophical foundations. In the wake of the modern crisis of reason, such a progression appears to have dead-ended in an impasse, which postmodern literature expresses in terms of disconnection between writing and historical significance. This also applies to the Italian context, despite its characteristic historicist and rationalist orientation. The idealist and Marxist approaches to history that dominated modern Italian culture – Croce's "straight road leading to 'liberty'" and the "gradual path" of dialectical materialism (Dalle Vacche 205) – have given way to a wandering mode. In Giulio Ferroni's words, "[i]l postmoderno (inteso nei suoi termini più generali come l'orizzonte determinante della cultura contemporanea) prende atto del fatto che la letteratura e le arti della tradizione sono giunte a un punto 'finale', che la comunicazione attuale ci colloca 'dopo' una storia che appare esaurita" (147). From this perspective, history appears as an immense reservoir for aimless practices of deconstruction and revision: "un'articolatissima costruzione pronta per essere 'decostruita', per essere rivoltata in tutte le sue connessioni, o più spesso per essere semplicemente riattraversata in lungo e in largo, in un viaggiare neutro, senza nessun possibile obbiettivo se non quello di riconfermare il presente, di ratificare la validità di un puro esserci" (Ferroni 147-48).

The "end of the journey" is a common trope for the negative conceptualization of history underlying such practices: the purposeful journey, traditional symbol of moral/epistemological direction, has turned into erratic wandering, which signals a seemingly terminal crisis of subjectivity: "la perdita di un centro e di una direzione dati per scontati nella dimensione istituzionale e massificata della cultura" (Marenco 8). Extrapolating from an image in Gianni Celati's essay, "Il bazar archeologico," writers at the end of the journey can be figured as jaded tourists who, tired of pursuing an illusory experience of exotic authenticity, limit themselves to idly browsing through a random display of lifeless objects, an "archeological bazaar." Such figures are especially prominent in recent travel literature, which dismantles "l'antica, totalizzante positività del racconto di viaggio, lo interiorizza, lo priva di mete e alla fine lo rivela inutile" (Marenco 7). This is, in my opinion, the genre that best displays the problematic implications of the end-of-the-journey mentality: an exoticist genealogy with its ideological ramifications – in particular, the Eurocentric, both "pessimistic and nostalgic evaluation (or devaluation) of modernity" that characterizes exoticism (Bongie 5). As I have argued elsewhere, such mentality bespeaks an inability or unwillingness to relinquish in full the fallen ideals of totalizing pursuits.[1]

---

[1] I have discussed this mentality and the relations between exoticism and postmodernism in "Incorporating the Exotic" and "Beyond 'the End of the Journey.'" My argument is premised on a genealogy of the decentered subject of postmodern theory as the last, disenfranchised heir in a long lineage of figures consecrated by colonialist and exoticist discourses: the explorer, embodying the ethnocentric arrogance of Western thought; the conqueror/colonizer, following in the footsteps of

Facing epistemological and moral bankruptcy, intellectuals at "the end of History" continue to perform on the familiar stage of decadence instead of pursuing riskier new roles. Though by negation rather than by affirmation – the one being the disillusioned reverse of the other, they remain anchored to the (now pulverized) notion of sovereign (united, authentic, authoritative) subjectivity, and thus inherit – in critical, "conscious" fashion – the melancholy, fetishistic attitude unselfconsciously embodied by the exoticist traveler of the past.[2]

That such an attitude plays a major role in contemporary Italian literature is confirmed by Gaia De Pascale's 2001 study, *Scrittori in viaggio*, which includes established authors like Alberto Arbasino, Gianni Celati, Giorgio Manganelli, Goffredo Parise, and Luigi Malerba as indicative of the latest tendency in travel writing. De Pascale ends her survey in a hopeful note, stating that the journey remains the symbol of a "passage from necessity to freedom which [. . .] cannot and must not come to an end" (240).[3] The

the explorer and enacting the aggressive, exploitative drives that the latter's knowledge authorizes; the belated, exoticist traveler, searching for an elusive fantasy of authenticity, and thus playing out the modern subject's division between a desire for progress through self-expansion/control and nostalgia for the myth of uncorrupted origins; and at the end of the journey, the deconstructed, anti-heroic protagonist of postmodernity, for whom the exotic Other remains the haunting memory of a mirage in a never-never land – the memory of what never was.

[2] See Bongie for an example of this "conscious," critical relationship with exoticism, and for a poignant analysis of fetishism and melancholia in exoticist literature. Drawing on Giorgio Agamben's interpretation of Freud, Bongie explains the function of the exotic Other by comparing it to the object of fetishist and melancholic desire: the object that "can never be found as it originally was (or more exactly, as it originally 'never was'). The only way that the fetishist can maintain the presence of the object that he desires is to invest in its absence" (76). Likewise, "[t]he melancholic confers reality upon an object that never was, mourning it, and thereby in a way giving life to its unreality" (196).

[3] All translations are mine. De Pascale summarizes the characteristics of the recent travel literature as follows: "Arbasino, Celati, Manganelli, Parise, Malerba e altri hanno, seppure in maniera diversa, rinunciato a 'insegnarci' il mondo, o meglio si sono proposti di mostrarci le menzogne del mondo così come viene comunemente pensato, contrapponendo

aforementioned authors, however, do not appear to support this positive interpretation of the trope. Paradoxically, in fact, they continue traveling/writing – as De Pascale notes – only to tell us "che non si può viaggiare più" (228). In the following pages, I will examine the implications of the negative notion of history at the heart of this paradox by focusing on the "wanderlust"[4] of a perceptive interpreter of the end-of-the-journey, Gianni Celati. I will then explore a challenging alternative to the postmodern impasse: the intellectual journey of Toni (Antonella) Maraini – a writer who, had she been included among the aforementioned *Scrittori in viaggio*, would have offered evidence in support of De Pascale's conclusion.[5] By her own

---

all'apparente linearità della realtà presentataci dai mass media 'un estremo uso della soggettività, una sfrontata professione di egotismo, una straripante presenza della personalità letteraria' [Pellegrino, *Verso oriente* 159] nonché un chiaro esempio del paradossale incontro tra un disincanto totale e un irrefrenabile impulso ad andare" (240).

[4] This term is used by West: "A great peripatetic, Celati has traveled extensively throughout Europe and North America, where he has done many public readings of his works; most recently, his wanderlust has taken him to West Africa" (xi). In the mid-1980s Celati left Italy and moved permanently to England. See West's monograph for a bio-bibliographical sketch and for the best study of Celati's work to date.

[5] A poet, novelist, art historian, and scholar of Maghreb, Toni Maraini has traveled extensively, especially in Morocco, where she lived from 1964 to 1986. Born in Tokyo during World War II, Maraini acquired a premature awareness of the precariousness of any "dimora" when her family was confined to a Japanese concentration camp (her parents – Fosco Maraini, an anthropologist, and Topazia Alliata, an artist – had refused to declare allegiance to the Repubblica di Salò). After the war Maraini left Japan (her "terra natia," *Ultimo tè a Marakesh* 92) as her family returned to Italy, where she never felt entirely "a casa": "Dal giorno della mia nascita sino ad oggi, le circostanze – e, poi, le scelte – mi hanno portata da un continente all'altro in luoghi che credevo dimore, ma dimore non erano. Erano passaggi, soggiorni, soste, pause, momenti di tregua col destino. Di tutti i distacchi [. . .] il primo è sempre rimasto vivido nei ricordi come un incubo tinto dai colori lividi della guerra, delle rovine, dell'inverno e del tramonto" (*Ultimo tè a Marakesh* 91). Maraini studied art history and cultural anthropology in Italy, England, the United States, and France. During her stay in Morocco – a "ciclo esperienziale" that she characterizes as a voluntary "'esilio' dall'occidente" (e-mail) – she was a cultural and social activist, taught at the University of Rabat, researched and wrote about the art, culture and traditions of Morocco, and published three collections of poems in

definition, she is a "viaggiatore a vita" (*Ultimo tè a Marakesh* 18), intent on finding "percorsi tra continenti" ("Lettera d'Occidente," *Poema d'Oriente*): a traveler who embraces a condition of "transumanza" rather than aimless wandering.

THE CONSUMMATE PERFORMANCE OF THE AIMLESS WANDERER

The sociopolitical conflict that erupted at the end of the Sixties, radically questioning the relevance of all cultural production, is one of the traumatic cruxes of the twentieth century that contributed to widening the perceived distance between literary culture and historical reality. Significantly, it is in the aftermath of the 1968 movement that Celati writes "Il bazar archeologico," arguing against the linear, monological discourse of history and defending a poetics of fragmentation, which he associates with an "archeological" perspective. Celati identifies the collector and the flâneur in Walter Benjamin's writings as paradigmatic embodiments of this perspective. The flâneur's aimless wandering through the "heterotopic" city and the collector's indiscriminate accumulation of heterogeneous "oggetti-ricordo" figure a departure from the totalizing, homogeneous continuity of history.[6] For

French. In Italy, along with numerous critical and scholarly essays, she has published a novel, *La murata*, a book of "racconti da una terra d'esilio" entitled *Ultimo tè a Marrakesh*, and two books of poetry, *Poema d'oriente* and *Le porte del vento*. Maraini currently lives and works in Rome.

[6] "La passione moderna del collezionismo è una *quête* di tracce del passato che dicano con il loro silenzio nel presente questa condizione tutta nuova dell'uomo che è l'essere senza origini. Nel bazar del collezionista tutto compare come flusso eteroclito, archeologico *bric-à-brac* di scarti, immagini frammentarie d'uno straniamento che può esprimersi solo con l'ecolalia del discorso folle, come in Eliot" (189-90). Bongie's considerations on the fetishist's compulsion also cast light on the collector's bazaar: "'Symbol of something and, at the same time, of its negation,' the fetish-object is always insufficient, since its presence signals the absence of the object that ought to be present – a fact that the fetishist himself cannot but be obscurely aware of and that explains his tendency 'to collect and multiply his fetishes.' The fetishist collects, to use Agamben's nice phrase, 'a harem of objects' that provide him with only a momentary satisfaction; to come to rest in any one of these objects would be to face up to the absence that inhabits it and that the

Celati, such a move appears to coincide with the definitive loss of any vantage point that would afford meaning, direction, and purpose to wandering and re-collection. He argues that the departure from the old vantage point opens the way to an alternative historical project: a "storia critica" (202), which ventures into areas neglected by monological, teleological discourse, searching for the objects that have been excluded, buried, forgotten as a result of history's arbitrary selection. However, he establishes narrow intellectual limits for this project, concluding that archeological discourse can tell us something only about the boundaries between the "normal" and "the extraneous," between the self and the other: "Su questi confini l'archeologia può dirci qualcosa; può decostruirli, mostrarne l'ordine rituale o convenzionale, le coazioni a ripetere, le retoriche normative. Ma piú in là di tanto non può andare, senza volerci dire cos'è l'estraneità *in sé*, senza diventare un'altra razionalizzazione dell'ignoto e dei suoi confini" (206; emphasis in original text). By Celati's definition, in keeping with the parameters of much postmodern discourse, the "storia critica" enabled by the archeological perspective thus amounts to a negation of history, "storia al negativo, antistoria," "metafora d'una perdita, d'un taglio dalle origini che incombe su ogni presente" (207).

Citing Claude Lévi-Strauss's denunciation of the system of projections through which the "civilized" man reduces extraneous cultures to his own rationality, motivations, and prejudices, Celati acknowledges that the archeological object may satisfy "il narcisismo e le manie estetiche dell'uomo normale," thus marking "un terreno vergine per future proiezioni di razionalità, progetti di acquisto e proiezione dell'uomo bianco adulto e normale" (205).7 But he claims that it is precisely "la denuncia di

---

fetishist is intent upon denying" (76-77). The distance between these two images, the collector's "bazaar" and the fetishist's "harem," obviously points to different levels of affective investment in the collected objects.

7 Celati refers, in particular, to the surrealists' fascination with the marginal, as illustrated by Breton's *Nadja*: "se Nadja è la figura quasi allegorica della marginalità rispetto alla vita normale, rispetto al progetto

questo genere di appropriazioni, insieme alla rivendicazione dell'oggetto quale traccia di un passato che nessuno
può indicare come 'suo', l'unica e fondamentale proposta
di ciò che continu[a] a chiamare il pensiero archeologico"
(205). Nevertheless, one can argue that his anti-historical
approach, spiraling into self-absorption, may also produce
forms of "acquisto e proiezione." Calvino presumably alluded to this very danger when he warned against "il
compiacimento dell'inesplicabile" in a related piece, "Lo
sguardo dell'archeologo," written in 1972 and published
in the collection *Una pietra sopra* (1980). Both Celati's essay and Calvino's "proposta di testo programmatico" were
conceived in preparation for the (unrealized) project of a
review (*Alì Babà*), which also included Carlo Ginzburg,
Enzo Melandri, and Guido Neri. Celati and Calvino move
from the same premise, taking stock of the crisis of the
traditional notion of history: "tutti i parametri, le catego-
rie, le antitesi che erano serviti per immaginare e classifi-
care e progettare il mondo sono in discussione" (Calvino
263). Unlike Celati's, however, Calvino's argument does
not preclude the possibility that the archeological approach – describing fragments, and avoiding to recompose
a prefigured "disegno," based on traditional concepts of
"Storia" and "Uomo" – may lead to new meaningful, albeit
precarious, vantage points: "il rifiuto di usare noi oggi qui
come spiegazione delle cose obbligherà alla fine le cose a
spiegare noi oggi qui" (264). In a later study inspired by
the same project, "Spie. Radici di un paradigma indiziario"
(1979), Ginzburg takes this constructive approach further
and theorizes an epistemological paradigm based on
traces and minimal clues ("un metodo interpretativo im-
perniato sugli scarti, sui dati marginali, considerati come
rivelatori," 65), through which he aims to overcome the
current "crisis of reason" ("uscire dalle secche della con-
trapposizione fra razionalismo e irrazionalismo," 59).
When we compare the prospects envisioned by these three
authors in regards to the same problematics, it becomes

---

stesso della normalità, non è anche allo stesso tempo la cavia di cui ci si
serve per capire dov'è questo limite e contemplare affascinati il pre-
cipizio?" (204-05).

apparent that Celati's theoretical elaborations present a more gloomy image of the Western intellectual's crisis, projecting it as a pervasive, terminal condition.[8] The self-reflective attitude underlying Celati's negative approach to history is exposed by the encounter with extraneous cultures in *Avventure in Africa*, the diary of his 1997 trip to Mali, Senegal, and Mauritania. Celati seeks to avoid the pitfalls of appropriation and projection by self-consciously reducing descriptions of local color to a bare minimum, and by consistently adopting an ironic perspective. He humorously comments on and debunks his pretensions to a rational understanding of the Other, as well as the fictions or fantasies that are born of desires and feelings – "tutte le intensità che 'touch and affect.'"[9] Yet, even such an ironic stance toward rationalist and exoticist fictions can produce alienating, essentializing, and ultimately self-serving images of Africa. Pondering on the failed purpose of the trip (his travel companion had planned a documentary on Dogon healing practices), the narrator concludes that the anthropologist's gaze should be turned onto "the people of tourists," since there is not much left to do with "le popolazioni primitive, ridotte a

---

[8] Celati writes on the debate generated by the "Alì Babà" project and on his relationship with Calvino in "Il progetto Alì Babà trent'anni dopo." West calls attention to the importance of this debate as an episode "marking the decisive move from the modern to the postmodern" (151). While underscoring the close relationship between Celati and Calvino, West also notes the distance that separated their views: "Perhaps the quality that most distanced Celati and Calvino from each other was the embrace of that 'dark whole' [the whole in our soul, the dark that we have inside of us] by the former, and the search for geometric clarity by the latter" (152).

[9] Celati notes that the same ideological system of control and indiscretion, the same mechanism of distancing and exploitation are at play in anthropological studies, in colonial exoticism, and in stories of "adventurous travels" (40). He uses the phrase "tutte le intensità che 'touch and affect'" in another essay, "Finzioni occidentali," defining the relationship between romance and affective energy: "Il romanzesco è la scoperta d'una dimensione di intensità libere, la violenza che risulta dal desiderio, il terrore che sorge dalla fascinazione, tutte le intensità che 'touch and affect' come si diceva nella prefazione a Prévost: è l'esperienza straordinaria vivibile solo a quel limite che è il corpo, perché il corpo sta oltre le soglie rituali della società" (28).

sbandati straccioni o comparse esotiche" (162-63).
Throughout the text, in fact, the African people are fragile
mirror opposites of the West ("extras" impersonating pre-
modern alterity), when they are not already the disinte-
grated mirror images of the Western syndrome of postmodernity, which Celati figures as an inexorable process
of fragmentation and "pulverization."[10] The most poignant
illustration of this point is the episode in which the narrator comments on his abrupt departure from Batouly (a
troubled, Westernized Senegalese woman who befriended
him), explaining that the senseless performance of good
feelings is, for him, "the most false": "l'ho vista andare
completamente a pezzi, come se avesse un braccio sul
comò, una gamba sul letto, la testa per terra. Volevo toc-
carle le dita rimaste per aria, dire cose affettuose, ma inutile pronunciare le nostre frasi insensate. Via da tutto, il
taxi aspettava, quando faccio l'uomo buono è la recita più
falsa" (175-76). Such a splitting of the authorial persona –
as at once a performer and a spectator – is a recurrent
narrative strategy that produces effects of emotional de-
tachment. This passage, in particular, shows how a self-
reflective perspective reduces extraneous cultures to
props for the Western intellectual's defeatist performance
– a *recita consumata* of his epistemological, moral, and
affective bankruptcy (*consumata* both in the sense of
"consummate" and "worn-out").

The intellectual's melancholic performance, in my
view, is the ultimate reversal (and consequence) of the ra-
tionalistic utopia. Frustrated in its ambition of total control, reason abdicates any constructive function and
safely limits its role to that of a defensive, debunking
mechanism. From this perspective, the self-imposed limits
of the postmodern writer appear to be a residual mani-
festation of the anti-sentimental bias of "serious" modern
narrative, which, as Celati himself notes in another essay
("Finzioni occidentali"), has tended to control emotional

---

[10] Dust and fog are pervasive images in Celati's writings. See for
instance the short story "Nella nebbia e nel sonno," *Cinema naturale* 40-
59.

involvement and identification, shunning "fantasia e sentimento" as characteristic of romance, and as appealing to intellectually "weak" readers ("ai giovani, alle donne, al volgo come categoria generica dei naturalmente diseducati," 19). Celati here quotes the eighteenth-century polemics against senseless, dangerous fictions, which sanctioned the split between two distinct genres: the novel, "promosso come adeguato ai pricipi conoscitivi sui quali la civiltà occidentale si va orientando," and romance, "respinto e tenuto per forma inadeguata alle conquiste conoscitive avvenute" (5). What did, asks Celati, our culture marginalize with romance and in romance? And by the same token, what did "serious" narrative at once marginalize and exploit through distancing mechanisms such as rationalization, parody, and doubling of the figure of the narrator? His answer is "il sentimento": "ciò che resta singolare e non può essere fatto precetto, ciò che sfugge alla volontà di controllo, di centralizzazione – fenomeno di discentramento, fuga laterale dal sistema chiuso della consapevolezza, della famiglia dello stato, dell'educazione, dilagare della marginalità in territori che per legge antica spettano ai funzionari del potere centrale: il linguaggio e il discorso" (46).

It is not farfetched to draw a connection between Celati's analysis of the distancing mechanisms of "serious literature" and his anti-rhetorical, anti-sentimental "performance" in *Avventure in Africa*. The psychological underpinnings of this performance are exposed by the narrator's considerations on the Westerner's "staggering" ego. When the Western ambition to exercise control on the outside world must be relinquished, he notes, the "rigid acrobatics" of self-control take center stage:

Proprio perché i bianchi hanno sempre il problema di padroneggiare le situazioni, *il ciondolamento sciolto degli africani* per loro è impossibile, e nelle situazioni poco controllabili adottano il ripiego di *padroneggiare rigidamente se stessi*. Per i bianchi qui si tratta di viaggiare sui trampoli del proprio io in mezzo alla folla dei neri, i quali non hanno quel problema e fiutano il *traballante equilibrio dei bianchi*, pronti a sfruttarlo per cavarci qualche soldo. (135; emphasis added)

This passage contrasts the African and the Western way of moving in space and time, a leitmotif in the book. Offering an apparent escape from the West's alienating tensions and constraints, the "idle," "smooth" rhythm of African life – based on a meager economy of subsistence and a rich network of interactions – attracts the writer, who wishes to assimilate it as a model for his craft of storytelling:

> Io scrivo, perché volevo ricominciare a scrivere a mano, e il diario di viaggio serve a quello. Vorrei fare l'elogio dello scrivere a mano, anche soltanto per dire che la marea lentamente sta entrando nella piccola ansa di pietre vulcaniche, che il sole è circondato da cirri biancastri e tutto è opaco all'intorno. Anche soltanto per passare il tempo, senza avere fretta, lasciando che il tempo si intrecci con le frasi che vengono alla spicciolata, mentre il boy spazza il patio e guardo l'immobilità del cormorano. (140)

Even though the conditional "vorrei" marks the distance between desire and fulfillment, Celati presents the contemplation of a natural flow seemingly unaffected by history as his most meaningful African experience: "L'inclinazione del sole regola le cadenze di ogni mossa, come tropismi secondo le ore di luce. Io vorrei seguire ogni momento prendendo appunti, annotare tutto quello che posso, ma il ritmo vale più dei concetti per acchiappare il mondo" (33). Tellingly, however, he fails to visit places and people that might have added a conceptual and historical dimension to this natural cadence. Because of a lack of effort (and perhaps fear of disappointment), he never reaches Banani, "la Roma imperiale del paese dogon" (87), and never meets a famous "raccontatore nomade," who might have taught him an important lesson in storytelling ("come fa lui a recitare i racconti della sua gente. Curiosità professionale, sarebbe stato istruttivo," 121). Furthermore, when the encounter with the Other takes place, he is consistently on guard against both the presumption of rational understanding and the rhetoric of feelings. His most "comfortable" persona, in fact, remains that of a bewildered spectator behind a shielding glass: "In questo hôtel de l'Amitié almeno mi trovo bene a scrivere, sui bordi della piscina al mattino o al pomeriggio, perché il luogo ispira le osservazioni da *spettatore dietro un vetro*" (101; emphasis added).

In the variants of a protective glass and of an impermeable "scafandro" (11),[11] the image of an insulating screen consistently characterizes the defensive stance of the wandering traveler, who recognizes as such the old, arrogant pretense to a masterly gaze, without however replacing it with a humbler disposition to cross the threshold of the Other: "Sera dopo la marcia. Credo che il villaggio si chiami Endé, ma non ho voglia di chiedere, mi sono rassegnato a non capire molto di questi posti. Sera, ore 7. Cauta esplorazione d'una stradina del villaggio, con occhiate di traverso, senza varcare troppo la soglia rituale.[. . .] Quando torno dovrò dire che di questi villaggi non ho visto quasi niente, tutto quello che posso dire l'ho letto nel libro di Griaule" (86). One gets the sense that everything has already been written and shown, whether in a serious piece of literature or in a promotional documentary (the narrator's companion, in fact, half-seriously concludes: "Siamo stati dentro a un documentario turistico," 178). This is a recurrent theme of contemporary travel writing, which reinforces the notion that the screen separating the Westerner from the exotic Other, and more generally the subject from the real world, is standard equipment for the inescapable "documentary of global simulation" in which we now live (179).

Mistrusting the delusions of both reason and emotion, and fearing a lapse into the already-said and already-seen, Celati abstains from the effort to recompose the meaning of his story in a "disegno complessivo."[12] Thus,

---

[11] See, for instance, the episode in which the narrator feels threatened by a surge of emotion upon witnessing Batouly's neurotic rage: "Il cortile è il suo territorio, ma fuori da quel territorio per lei Dakar è un inferno. Allora quando ci pensa diventa una bestia in gabbia, e brontola iraconda, e va a pezzi. Davanti a simili casi il turista europeo si smarrisce, come in stato di assedio dietro il suo vetro protettivo" (138).

[12] This is a quote from Calvino's "Presentazione" to *Una pietra sopra* (viii). Calvino presents his collection of essays spanning twenty-five years as a story with a "comprehensive design," the story of his own growing perplexities about the intellectual's role as an interpreter/guide of historical change, and of his tireless search for meaning: "Il personaggio

in closing his travelogues, he offers an existential lesson couched in negative terms:

> Ma poi si sa che quando uno è lasciato dietro un vetro, tende a sentire che gli manca qualcosa, anche se ha tutto e non gli manca niente, e questa mancanza di niente forse conta qualcosa, perché uno potrebbe anche accorgersi di non aver bisogno davvero di niente, tranne del niente che gli manca davvero, del niente che non si può comprare, del niente che non corrisponde a niente, il niente del cielo e dell'universo, o *il niente che hanno gli altri che non hanno niente.* (179; emphasis added)

The imponderable value to be discovered in Africa – the "something" that the narrator/traveler feels to be missing upon returning to Europe's picture-perfect world (the inevitable "documentario perpetuo" in which you see "tutto pulito, ordinato, levigato, glossy, flashing, rifatto a nuovo," 178-79) – predictably adds up to "nothing." Celati thus remains true to his poetic persona, the aimless wanderer. It is quite possible to interpret the final string of negatives as a litotes, an irony of dissimulation, in which case one can infer that this "nothing" is actually "everything."[13] In both the literal and the figurative reading,

---

che prende la parola in questo libro [. . .] entra in scena negli Anni Cinquanta cercando d'investirsi d'una personale caratterizzazione nel ruolo che allora teneva la ribalta: 'l'intellettuale impegnato'. Seguendo le sue mosse sul palcoscenico, s'osserverà come in lui, visibilmente anche se senza scosse brusche, l'immedesimazione in questa parte viene a meno a poco a poco col dissolversi della pretesa d'interpretare e guidare un processo storico. Non per questo si scoraggia l'applicazione a cercar di comprendere e indicare e comporre. [. . .] È ponendosi come esperienza conclusa che la successione di queste pagine comincia a prendere una forma, a diventare una storia che ha il suo senso nel disegno complessivo" (viii).

[13] For West, Celati's African travelogues in general, and the conclusion in particular, warrant a more positive interpretation: "With this play on the word 'nothing,' which is transformed from a negative lack to a positive quality of union with the freely given sky and world around us [. . .] Celati closes his Notebooks, written in the state of grace that aimless wandering can sustain and money cannot buy: Travel is a shedding – of possessions, of self, of pretensions, of preconceptions – and writing is a light trace of the blessed 'nothing' that remains" (268).

however, meaning and value remain equally beyond reach, like those elusive "others that have nothing."

From the viewpoint of the poststructuralist and post-metaphysical discourses that have played a central role in Western academia over the past three decades, a poetics of idle wandering such as the one informing *Avventure in Africa* may appear to be the safest antidote to the ambitious and arrogant strivings of the old phallic order.[14] There are however – as Calvino's archeological project, for instance, shows – more purposeful ways of wandering away from the old order. I am especially interested in the new *percorsi* traced by women writers, which overall remain in need of critical attention. In a larger project currently in progress, I seek to address this need by examining how some recent women's works published in Italy refigure the trope of the journey and, in so doing, confront the impasse of postmodernity. As I have argued above, a crucial aspect of the impasse is a negative notion of historical memory that points to an intricate relationship between exoticism and postmodernism. Toni Maraini's writings are especially relevant to this aspect of my study. In order to trace paths between seemingly distant cultures and separate realms of experience, her eccentric practice of intellectual *transumanza* in fact refigures history through the exotic, crossing the conceptual boundaries of postmodernism.

WRITING IN/AS TRANSHUMANCE

Maraini is both sharply critical of the self-absorbed stance prevalent in contemporary Western discourse, and committed to (re)connecting the heritage of Western culture with that of a land she views as "un frammento della

---

[14] Affinities can be noted, in particular, between Celati and the practitioners of so-called "pensiero debole." See West 13, 31, 39, 41, 70-71, and 146. West considers Celati's "craft" of storytelling in the context of "anti-phallic writing": a melancholic response to the perceived failures of the phallic discourses of domination and linear progress that infused modernity; a permanent state of convalescing from the disease of ambitious striving, glory-seeking, and the delirium of intentions.

patria universale."[15] The poems and narratives inspired by her experience of intellectual exile actually reveal a poetics of the fragment that, like Celati's archeological perspective, can be characterized as postmodern. Maraini is concerned with similar metaliterary issues, and consistently examines the premises and limits of her own writing. But she figures her work as a painstaking mosaic in progress, rather than a random collection of archeological objects, and thus conveys a constructive notion of memory and history. How does this project confront the impasse of post- or anti-history? I believe that Maraini negotiates it by immersing herself, both intellectually and emotionally, in the complex, fluid worlds of other cultures. She approaches them with discretion, and yet without shields against the *intensità affettive* that such immersions inevitably generate. (I have in mind, by contrast, the image of the "scafandro," which in Celati's book figures the Westerner's insulation.)

The physical, cultural, and mental journey that Maraini describes moves in different dimensions, uncovering buried links and tracing fresh ones:

> Quando sono venuta in Marocco, ho dato le spalle all'Occidente. Ho cercato di viaggiare con circospezione nei tre livelli menzionati (paese altrui, storia personale, vita immaginativa) lasciandomi portare dagli eventi. Questi eventi includevano anche il *dirsi* attraverso quei momenti della storia occidentale che servivano da ponte con l'esperienza *ad Oriente* (*Anno 1424*, Saggio sulle poetesse provenzali). (Maraini and Camboni 219; emphasis in original)

As Maraini explains in a 1983 "dialogo" with Marina Camboni, her journey's goal is "liberare l'esotismo" (Maraini and Camboni 220), in other words, to break free from its trappings: the accretions that have ossified the image of the Orient as a mythical, a-historical space – the elsewhere of desire. Such liberation can be attained by revers-

---

[15] This phrase appears in the blurb on the cover of the second edition of *Ultimo tè a Marrakesh*, to which all quotes refer.

ing the traditional exoticist perspective, by searching for this imaginary space in the depths of Western consciousness/ history, while at the same time recognizing the historicity of the real Orient:

> Con la morte dell'Oriente alla Nerval, e con il risorgimento dell'Oriente reale (che è anche un affiorare risorgivo al livello della nostra coscienza dato che l'Oriente reale, storico/ politico e molteplice, è sempre stato al suo posto), siamo obbligati da un lato a riflettere sull'Oriente reale e, dall'altro, a riconoscere nella nostra stessa civiltà la presenza di un' orientalità velata, censurata e in perpetuo eclissarsi. Siamo tenuti a fare spazio a un essere-oriente implicito nel divenire dialettico della cultura. Se si indaga sulla storia occidentale si trova questo "movimento dell'essere-a-oriente", senza il quale d'altronde non sarebbe potuto esistere quel continuo riassesto (attraverso le eresie, i movimenti di idee, etc.) necessario per non degenerare nella "fuga verso la realtà" (termine usato in psicanalisi da Winnicot), patologica quanto la "fuga dalla realtà". Io non penso tanto qui alla nozione nietzschiana di una polarità apollineo-dionisiaca che separa e frammenta nell'antitesi, ma a un Apollo agitato dal suo essere-Dioniso, o viceversa, in fertile intimità e equilibrio." (Maraini and Camboni 220)

The Orient that Maraini (re)cognizes is thus a fertile interfusion of the rational and the irrational surfacing at various points in Western thought – in Renaissance hermetic Neoplatonism for instance, which derived from oriental wisdom the idea that the root of truth lies only in poetry.

While mindful of the violence that may underlie utopian thinking, Maraini denounces the superficiality and sterility of postmodern "eclecticism," assuming the role of an active witness of/in history: "nessuna problematica estetica può farmi dimenticare che è dovere di scrittore testimoniare per la dignità dell'umano" (e-mail).[16] To be

---

[16] In her poem "Esilio errante" Maraini refers to a "palindromica Utopia / in perpetuo stato d'assenza" (*Poema d'oriente*). She explains this image as follows: "la 'palindromica utopia' è quella che, vissuta in qualsivoglia maniera o direzione lungo la curva del tempo, rimane pur tuttavia sempre uguale e non muta: un'utopia pienamente significante e infinita.

an active witness, for Maraini, means to engage both in sociopolitical causes (such as volunteering for needy children) and in "a perennial hermeneutic art" ("lavorare sul libro dei Libri del mondo," Maraini and Camboni 220) a project which she sustains through a variety of sources: most notably, Arab philosophy and literature, Mediterranean mythology, the esoteric and mystic currents in Western culture, and contemporary psychoanalysis. Her writings thus compose a "mosaic" of the multifaceted world she explored, and became attached to, loosing and finding herself in Morocco.

The mosaic is a central figure in *Poema d'Oriente*. It defines individual poems that compose the "summary" of a personal journey: "tornare indietro / (sans remettre les pieds dans les mêmes trous) / riassumersi in un corto poema / (mosaico)" ("Mosaico II"); and it points to a "structuring impulse" in the collection, which emerges as the overarching design of a message to the reader: an invitation to travel "nel pensarsi del poema" ("Invito"), and share the poet's laborious dream – her unrelenting effort to invent the world ("È stato detto che").[17] The poetic

---

È diversa dalle utopie lineari nel senso che non nasce e non muore, non si consuma con le disillusioni dell'esperienza ma serve da guida tutta la vita. Una sorta di stella polare dell'animo. Il mio è certo, per forza di cose, per scelta e per legge di destino, un percorso alternativo, ma questa utopia mia interagisce con tante altre sul piano di quel 'communicative ethics' o 'interactive universalism' che lei menziona [this is a reference to an e-mail by the author] e che ci sostiene in tante, tanti, tantissimi a dare futuro al mondo. Come ha scritto Gaston Bachelard (un altro autore che, con Gilbert Durand, mi ha influenzata): bisogna sognare il mondo per farlo esistere. Allora, tante utopie messe insieme possono sognare un mondo migliore. La creazione letteraria ha molto da fare con questa faccenda di sogni! La mia opera è tutta lì" (e-mail).

[17] As reported by Keala Jewell (*The Poiesis of History* 11), in a paper delivered at Dartmouth College ("The Mosaic of Metastructure," March 1989) Rebecca West has used the term *mosaic* to describe a "structuring impulse" in lyric collections that "attempt to overcome Symbolist and Hermetic poetics by inserting fragments into an implicit teleology." Jewell takes stock of such structuring impulse in her analysis of three authors, Bertolucci, Luzi and Pasolini. She studies "the ways in which these three poets mix poetic forms associated in the cultural tradition with certain forms of consciousness – namely epic and lyric – in order to

journey is at times discursively recounted (as in "Quando ero giovane" and "In un pomeriggio di fine primavera"), other times fragmentarily and hermetically evoked (as in "Frammenti dal manoscritto di Samarcanda" and "Verso Sud: oltre Agzd"). The image of the mosaic thus also refers to another salient feature of the collection: a style "fragmented" by citations, word play, parentheses, and the recourse to various generic forms, which complicates meaning without precluding it. The fact that the collection is presented as a *poema* underscores the narrative and didactic dimensions of the mosaic: the autobiographical "journey" and the ethical/political message that it evinces. With regard to the Italian context, this poetic practice can be linked to both a visionary/lyrical and an experimental lineage: by Maraini's own account, Dino Campana played an important role in her formative years, along with Amelia Rosselli and Emilio Villa (e-mail). One can additionally relate the mosaic of *Poema d'Oriente* to the "*poiesis* of history" investigated by Keala Jewell in her homonymous book: a study of innovative post-war poetry that strove to connect the private world of lyric to the world of history by experimenting with "archaic or outdated genres" (3) – genres such as the *poema*, which evokes a powerful Italian tradition of epic and didactic verse.[18] Maraini's poetic horizons, however, extend well beyond Italian poetry, her acknowledged influences ranging from French surrealism to Sufi mysticism.[19]

The short narratives in *Ultimo tè a Marrakesh* also create a "mosaico d'oriente," which combines autobiographical memories, intertextual references, theoretical considerations, political arguments, and images of the landscape – physical and cultural. These various frag-

---

reconceptualize the relations of history and poetry," dispelling "the critical cliché that 'civic' verse' must be narrative and realistic" (x).

[18] As Jewell argues with regards to Pasolini, Bertolucci, and Luzi, the aforementioned tension between lyric fragmentation and antilyric narrativity/didacticism can be viewed as an attempt to figure historical becoming and disappearance in poetry (245).

[19] See Camboni for a perceptive analysis of motifs from Arab philosophy and literature in Maraini's early poetry.

ments are embedded in stories of meaningful encounters, and the collection of stories is presented as the "Dépliant borderline" of an idiosyncratic travel agency, inviting the readers to follow the example of the writer/traveler/ guide, and to accept Morocco's hospitality:

> In Marocco, siamo partiti dalla preistoria e dai guadi pietrificati del Sahara, abbiamo camminato per raggiungere le mille incisioni rupestri del Monte Yagu, il cromlech di Mzora, la valle di Fumm al Hassan dalle scritture paeo-berbere e tanti altri luoghi per risalire, millennio dopo millennio, secolo dopo secolo, dall'epoca pre-islamica a quella islamica, dalla dimensione sahariana a quella mediterranea, dagli inizi dei fermenti modernisti alle crisi delle nuove prospettive attuali e siamo giunti nel bel mezzo delle fragorose risate e dispute di un gruppo di artisti e poeti seduti a un caffè di Casablanca. Vi siamo stati ricevuti come un convitato d'altri tempi. Un bicchiere alla menta zuccherato ha sancito una recondita, tenace e sommersa comunanza. Il lungo periplo è stato istruttivo. Ci siamo ritrovati con più collaudate capacità di conoscenza. Non possiamo dare maggiori garanzie della nostra serietà. (15)

One of the experiences described in this quote, the conversation among commensals, is a recurrent narrative strategy in the book. Dialogues often cross cultural and temporal boundaries, evoking what a story defines as a "Convito d'ombre": "Frammentario e confuso. Un atto incompleto; sospeso a una moltitudine di atti mancanti. Un soliloquio senza epilogo. Un monologo con parvenza di dialoghi (tutti veridici pur tuttavia). Un racconto senza trama" (77).

The premise of this story ("Una risata transmoderna e neofutura, ovvero: il Convito d'ombre") is Pirandellian, recalling in particular "La tragedia di un personaggio": the author's mind becomes a room visited by phantasmatic figures. But Pirandello's ironic persona maintains the "professional" attitude of a doctor or lawyer towards the uninvited characters who, driven by an ideal of aesthetic completion, compete for his authorial attention. In contrast, the female narrator of Maraini's metapoetic tale allows herself to be overwhelmed by her guests, who voice memories of engaging, stimulating conversations. Despite or perhaps because of this surge of memories, she is able to overcome an impasse in her project: to talk about modernity by summoning a symposium of the wise, the ones who "portano verso il futuro un'eredità salvata da oblio, ignoranza, quotidiane traversie e inquisizioni" (62). Throughout this collection, as well as in other works, many cultural domains are embodied by Maraini's interlocutors: past and present protagonist of Arab intellectual history; the "common" people she encountered and befriended in her travels – repositories of the submerged history of Mediterranean syncretism; and Westerners who share both her "dissenso con l'Occidente" and her concern with the West's heritage – "una sorta di quintessenza alchemica. Una eredità funzionale, non contro tutti ma *con* tutti" (47; emphasis in original text). It is noteworthy that Maraini's use of memory reverses the paradigm embodied by the most metapoetic of Pirandello's unrealized characters, Dr. Fileno. This "tragic" figure advocates looking at the present through a distancing lens, as if it were long past, so as to minimize – to use again Celati's phrase – "tutte le intensità che 'touch and affect.'" Maraini's *convitati*, instead, make the past present so as to project the ancient roots of a shared heritage of values into the future.

Dr. Fileno can be added to the genealogy of symptomatic characters sketched by Calvino in his 1955 essay "Il midollo del leone," characters that personify the modern writer's alienation from the world ("il tema [. . .] della non-adesione, del rapporto negativo col mondo," 5). Having identified this pervasive intellectual malaise, Calvino proceeds to give a prescription for a new literature deeply rooted in the past:

> In un articolo di Gramsci abbiamo trovato, citata da Romain Rolland, una massima di sapore stoico e giansenista adottata come parola d'ordine rivoluzionaria: "pessimismo dell'intelligenza, ottimismo della volontà." La letteratura che vorremmo veder nascere dovrebbe esprimere nella acuta intelligenza del negativo che ci circonda la volontà limpida e attiva che muove i cavalieri negli antichi cantari o gli esploratori nelle memorie di viaggi settecentesche.
> Intelligenza, volontà: già proporre questi termini vuol dire credere nell'individuo, rifiutare la sua dissoluzione.[. . .]
> Vorremmo anche noi inventare figure di uomini e di donne

pieni d'intelligenza, di coraggio, e d'appetito, ma mai entusiasti, mai soddisfatti, mai furbi o superbi. (15)

Calvino acknowledges (albeit reluctantly, for fear of falling into "schematizzazioni sociologiche," 7) that the only examples pointing in this courageous direction are female characters and characters created by women writers: "i pochi esempi di risolutezza intellettuale o morale o d'azione li troviamo nei personaggi femminili di alcuni nostri scrittori, e li troviamo con molta frequenza, ora realizzati poeticamente, ora solo sul piano delle intenzioni, nei libri delle scrittrici" (7). The source of the moral strength he seeks, however, is not contained within a particular ideology or movement. It is the "marrow" of all true poetry (a term by which he refers to literature in general): "in ogni poesia vera esiste un midollo di leone, un nutrimento per una morale rigorosa, per una padronanza della storia" (17). Forsaking the historical legacy of literary tradition amounts, for Calvino, to a senseless act of self-mutilation: "Un certo atavico senso del risparmio, acuito dalla coscienza di vivere in un'epoca di dissennato spreco, ci impone di non amputarci la minima parte di noi stessi, e di cercare d'utilizzare il più possibile di ciò che sta alle nostre spalle" (17).

In this fundamental respect, Maraini's message concurs with the lesson offered by Calvino:[20] they both envision writing as a never-ending effort to approach the real, a journey sustained by a vital cultural heritage. But for Maraini an additional goal is of paramount importance: to shift the parameters of such heritage. Gender is one of the parameters to be reconsidered, but is not the central axis of the shift she pursues.[21] While searching Western

---

[20] Calvino is one of the few modern Italian writers whom Maraini mentions in response to my question about her formation (the others are Luigi Pirandello, Dino Campana, Amelia Rosselli, and Emilio Villa). She describes her formation as predominantly shaped by foreign authors and, through her studies in art history and cultural anthropology, by encounters with the most disparate cultures (e-mail).

[21] In "Palinsesto," an essay that she describes as a "mosaic" in progress, composed of variously dated fragments, Maraini addresses the

tradition for its "veiled, censured" *orientalità*, which is often embodied as *femminilità*, she moves to the margins of the contemporary Western intellectual world and its many -isms. Her notion of historical memory does not rest, therefore, in an easily definable location. She can be viewed as postmodern in as much as this term – taken in a broad sense – stands for critical distance from the failures and excesses of Western modernity. However, even though she addresses metatextual concerns commonly associated with Western, poststructuralist discourses, Maraini is not a postmodernist in the sense that she adheres to any such version of postmodernism. In this narrower sense, postmodernism emphasizes the deconstruction of reason, identity, and history, positing a radical divide between the logocentric tradition and post-metaphysical thought – a boundary beyond which any universalist ideal appears as an illusion to be exposed. Maraini is also committed to a critique of Western universalist theories. But she rejects the wholesale deconstruction of preexisting knowledge, and looks skeptically at categories of periodization like "postmodernity" and "post-*histoire*," which may fail to recognize the historical claims of non-Western others ("le stesse quotidiane aspirazioni alla giustizia, alla felicità, al sapere e al progresso del resto del mondo," e-mail). Rather than just maintain a critical distance from all cultural identities, she reaches for the best in different cultures and traditions, including the universalist moral and political legacy of the Enlightenment.[22] She advances a notion of exile comparable to

---

relationship between *sesso* and *scrittura* as an unresolved question: "È questo itinerario di riflessione, così com'è presentato qui in frammenti annotati a mano e in brani cancellati, sintomatico di uno dei tanti percorsi possibili del pensarsi della *scrittura*? E devo forse aggiungere '*al femminile*' o '*di donna*'? O mi basta appropriarmi dell'intuizione Freudiana della creazione come '*testo significante senza bisogno d'autore*' e citare la frase di Julia Kristeva '*la scrittura ignora il sesso*' o quella di Diotima di Mantinea a Socrate nel 'Convito' di Platone '*tutti siamo, o Socrate, gravidi nel corpo e nella mente*'?" (106).

[22] The following is an excerpt from Maraini's response to my question concerning her approach to history: "In sostanza ho capito che la Storia c'è, ha fasi, periodi, involuzioni/evoluzioni, procede secondo dinamiche e

Seyla Benhabib's theorization of the social critic's exile as
the utopian space of an "interactive universalism": a
space of negotiation between the postmodernist critique
and the universalist tradition, in which Benhabib explores
her project of "communicative ethics" (226-28). More generally, Maraini can be associated with writers described
by Caren Kaplan as "men and women who move between
the cultures, languages, and the various configurations of
power and meaning in complex postcolonial situations
[and who] possess what Chela Sandoval calls 'oppositional
consciousness,' the ability to read and write culture on
multiple levels" (187).

It is precisely by sustaining an oppositional consciousness with a communicative ethics that Maraini can infuse
the postmodern poetics of the fragment with a dynamic,
constructive view of historical memory. As she suggests in

strutture ovunque presenti, muta e va avanti a spirale, ma non muore.
Forse può esistere una Storia senza esseri umani, ma non può esistere
una umanità senza Storia . . . È nel nostro DNA. La prova l'ho avuta
proprio dalle mie riflessioni in campo socio-antropologico; nelle mie
ricerche sul terreno, in archivio e nel lavoro di critica bibliografica di
quanto era stato scritto sul Marocco ho potuto provare come – negando
la Storia degli Altri non occidentali sotto la pressione dell'ideologia
coloniale – l'antropologia occidentale si fosse drammaticamente sba-
gliata. In Marocco la Storia riemergeva da ogni documento, ogni realtà
quotidiana. Bastava applicare criteri di ricerca socio-economico-politici e
culturali 'non coloniali' ma universali. Osservata dai 'margini', tutto
questo era molto chiaro. I criteri storiografici occidentali erano parziali e
spesso mentivano (anche perché sempre scritti dalle stesse istanze
referenziali). Forse la supposta fine della Storia è la fine di UNA storia
scritta a una sola dimensione. Ma la Storia c'è. Eppure non è così
semplice capirlo. Viviamo una fase di negazione del concetto di Storia
perché le trasformazioni del vecchio concetto sono immense e trau-
matiche e non cogliamo cosa sta accadendo. Tuttavia, se prendiamo atto
del post-moderno o dell'anti o post-storico, si tratta pur sempre di 'fasi'
della Storia universale. Una fase che c'è, che ci condiziona, che
critichiamo, che cerchiamo di capire ma che non ci autorizza a negare
quanto ci precede. [. . .] Noi usiamo materiali o frammenti delle epoche
passate (Illuminismo etc.) credendo che siamo materiali morti ma non è
così. Il post-moderno può essere utile in quanto strumento o esperienza
per maturare una posizione critica rispetto all'idea totalitaria di Storia e
per decostruire tante menzogne della modernità, anzi della moderniz-
zazione e dell'eurocentrismo. Ma questo non significa negare quanto
rimane materiale utile e fondante, e quanto è conquista inalienabile
dell'esperienza e del sapere" (e-mail).

23

"Poema d'Oriente," texts are composed with fragmentary, and even illusory materials; yet every single text can be a unique *percorso* contributing to the human journey in progress, "il divenire della coscienza":[23]

> Ogni poema d'oriente è anche poema d'esilio
> sempre in ricerca va dove nasce il mattino
> ma dov'è l'oriente di un luogo e l'occidente dell'altro?
> chiedeva chi viaggia e cercava i suoi passi lontani:
> nessun ritorno sui passi è mai avvenuto,
> ogni poema è sempre percorso a parte
> ogni poema è frammento di un testo che migra
> la storia sarebbe altrimenti statica forma
> e la parola prigione di incomunicabili segni.
> (*Poema d'Oriente*)

These lines illustrate some of the themes discussed above. They present the Orient as the poetic space where an individual "percorso" can become part of a shared heritage, as a fragment of a text in progress ("frammento di un testo che migra"). By making this Orient her destination, the poet chooses an existence of exile, a destiny that in Maraini's writing does not signify a static condition of alienation, but an assiduous search for "comunicabili segni": "le strutture dell'immaginarsi del mondo" (Maraini and Camboni 215), "l'eterna comune umanità in cammino nella stessa storia" (*Ultimo tè a Marrakesh* 12)

If her first collection of poems (*Message d'une migration*) may appear to move away from the West in search of Oriental roots, later works clearly show that this movement is not a definitive flight from Western culture (and the old "self"), but a persistent wandering through different dimensions. To (re)cognize the Other, we must – as Julia Kristeva puts it – become "strangers to ourselves," and open paths between dimensions that have been segregated by the Western symbolic order. Maraini aptly defines this way of wandering as "transumanza," connot-

---

[23] A call to be part of "il divenire della coscienza" is the ultimate message of Maraini's novel, *Anno 1424*. Quote refers to the second edition, *La murata* 164. On this novel, see Blum, "Toni Maraini's *vivere vagabondo*" 326-32, and Camboni 209-12.

ing a cyclic change of terrenes and search for vital suste-
nance: "Ogni incursione in territori diversi mi ha arric-
chita. In questo senso io parlerei più di una 'transumanza'. Nel senso che, come nella transumanza, si tratta
di un continuo vai e vieni, di un attraversamento alla
scoperta di qualcosa e poi di un ritorno a se stessi" (e-
mail).

Maraini's latest collection, *Le porte del vento*, continues to effect such a "continuo vai e vieni." Opening into
the "millenarie mescolanze" of collective memory, which
the West's gates obstinately shut out ("Le porte d'occidente"),[24] some poems evoke oneiric gardens ("I giardini
del tempo"), and are animated by winds and birds whose
messages blend with the soul's "whispering" ("Ascoltare il
vento"). Other poems, instead, bear stark witness to pain-
ful divisions, tracing a "map of the sorrow" brought about
by the stormy "violence of history" ("La mappa del dolore,"
"Allora"). The last suite suggests that these projects are
deeply connected, as they ultimately point to the same
origin and vantage point: Maraini writes from within "the
womb of the world" ("Da dentro il ventre del mondo"). The
poet's reverie, in fact, did not shut the door in reality's
face: "non ho lasciato fuori il mondo: / *lo ascolto come da
dentro il suo ventre*" (67; emphasis in original). Conversely,
in finally choosing "the concreteness of life," she opens
the door to a renewed dialogue with the wind, the
spiritual force that inspired her poetic dream: "allora ho
detto: voglio tornare / alla concretezza della vita / voglio
incamminarmi fuori dalla poesia // *e ho ricominciato / a
parlare col vento*" (70; emphasis in original).

CONCLUSION

"Each epoch has its own 'poetics of History'," writes
Jewell quoting Hayden White's phrase, "and according to
a dialectics of these, human history unfolds – or at least

---

[24] "Le porte d'occidente si chiudono / ai limiti di frontiere testarde /
ferite ricoprono ferite / strati di cenere sugli animi / le porte d'occidente
si chiudono / senza più sapere dove / nasce l'occidente e dove muore //
ma non sopravviverà un mondo / ripulito di memorie / non sopravviverà
senza / le sue millenarie / mescolanze."

attains some configuration for the present" (244). Continuing to assume, as was done over the past two centuries, that history unfolds in interrelation with *"poiesis as a making,"*[25] we can conclude that Celati's "discorso archeologico" and Maraini's "epopea di memorie" exemplify the dialects through which some configuration for our present can be attained. On the one hand, the approach "from the margins" that informs Maraini's mosaic in progress negotiates the postmodern impasse and advances the notion of a vital relationship between writing and history. Celati's archeological bazaar, on the other hand, figuring "una *quête* senza meta, spazializzazione e *flânerie*," conveys the Eurocentric sense of being "dopo la fine," " 'dopo' una storia che sembra esaurita" (Ferroni 148). Together, these two different emplotments of historical consciousness point to a configuration of irreducible mobility and multiplicity, which may be both dispiriting and inspiring. As Celati notes, "nelle figure di finzione l'importanza sta nella peripezia attraverso cui ci portano, la danza a cui ci persuadono, i movimenti a cui ci conducono." Ultimately, it depends on the traveler/ writer's disposition whether or not such a fluid, heterogeneous configuration impels, in De Pascale's words, to a "passage from necessity to freedom which [. . .] cannot and must not come to an end."

WORKS CITED

Benhabib, Seyla. *Situating the Self: Gender, Community and Postmodernism in Contemporary Ethics.* New York: Routledge, 1992.

Blum, Cinzia Sartini. "Toni Maraini's *vivere vagabondo*: Exile as the Last Utopia. *Annali d'Italianistica* 20 (2002): 325-42.

---

[25] "[T]hroughout the nineteenth century, as well as the twentieth, the epochs of history continued to be viewed as closely related to *poiesis* as a making, to aesthetic history, to the history of human creations" (Jewell 244). Jewell refers to Hegel, Marx, and Nietzsche as examples of different emplotments of historical consciousness, which however share a view of history as inextricably associated with human creations.

____. "Beyond 'the End of the Journey': Biancamaria Frabotta's Writing from *Fuga* to *Viandanza*." Forthcoming in *Italian Culture*.

____. "Incorporating the Exotic: From Futurist Excess to Postmodern Impasse." Forthcoming in *A Place in the Sun: Italian Colonial Culture from the Post Unification Period to the Present*. Ed. Patrizia Palumbo. University of California Press.

Bongie, Chris. *Exotic Memories: Literature, Colonialism, and the Fin de Siècle*. Stanford: Stanford University Press, 1991.

Calvino, Italo. *Una pietra sopra. Discorsi di letteratura e società*. Turin: Einaudi, 1980.

Camboni, Marina. "Volo a Oriente. Le opere di Toni Maraini." *L'esotismo nelle letterature moderne*. Ed. Elémire Zolla. Rome: Liguori, 1983. 208-13.

Celati, Gianni. "Finzioni occidentali." *Finzioni occidentali: Fabulazione, comicità e scrittura*. Turin: Einaudi, 1986. 5-49.

____. "Il bazar archeologico." *Finzioni occidentali: Fabulazione, comicità e scrittura*. Turin: Einaudi, 1986. 187-215. First published in *Il Verri* 12 (1975): 11-35.

____. *Avventure in Africa*. Milan: Feltrinelli, 1998.

____. "Il progetto Alì Babà trent'anni dopo." *Riga* 14 (1998): 313-21.

____. *Cinema naturale*. Milan: Feltrinelli, 2001.

Dalle Vacche, Angela. *The Body in the Mirror: Shapes of History in Italian Cinema*. Princeton: Princeton University Press, 1992.

De Pascale, Gaia. *Scrittori in viaggio. Narratori e poeti italiani del Novecento in giro per il mondo*. Turin: Bollati Boringhieri, 2001.

Ginzburg, Carlo. "Spie. Radici di un paradigma indiziario." *Crisi della ragione*. Ed. Carlo Gargani. Turin: Einaudi, 1979. 57-106.

Jewell, Keala. *The Poiesis of History: Experimenting with Genre in Postwar Italy*. Ithaca and London: Cornell University Press, 1992.

Kaplan, Caren. "Deterritorializations: The Rewriting of Home and Exile in Western Feminist Discourse." *Cultural Critique* 6 (Spring 1987): 187-98.

Kristeva, Julia. *Strangers to Ourselves*. New York: Columbia University Press, 1991.

Maraini, Toni.

____. *Message d'une Migration: Poème 1970-1975*. Casablanca: Shoof Publications, 1976.

____. *Le Récit de l'Occultation: Devoilement*. Casablanca: Shoof Publications, 1982.

____. *Phantasmata Diwan*. Casablanca: Al Asas, 1987.

____. "Palinsesto." *Donne e scrittura*. Ed. Daniela Corona. Palermo: La Luna, 1990. 105-33.

____. *La murata. Romanzo*. Palermo: La Luna, 1991. Rpt. of *Anno 1424*. Venezia: Marsilio, 1976.

____. *Poema d'Oriente*. Rome: Semar, 2000.

____. *Ultimo tè a Marrakesh e nuovi racconti*. Rome: Edizioni Lavoro, 2000. Expanded ed. of *Ultimo tè a Marrakesh. Racconti.* 1994.

____. E-mail to the author, 6 Aug. 2002.

____. *Le porte del vento. Poesie 1995-2002*. San Cesario di Lecce: Manni, 2003.

Maraini, Toni and Marina Camboni. "L'esotico e l'esilio. Dialogo con Marina Camboni." *L'esotismo nelle letterature moderne*. Ed. Elémire Zolla. Rome: Liguori, 1983. 214-27.

Marenco, Franco. "Premessa: Scritture infedeli." *"Fine dei viaggi": spazio e tempo nella narrazione moderna*. Spec. issue of *L'Asino d'oro* 1.1 (May 1990): 5-8.

Pellegrino, Angelo. *Verso oriente. Viaggi e letteratura degli scrittori italiani nei paesi orientali (1912-1982)*. Rome: Istituto dell'Enciclopedia Treccani, 1985.

West, Rebecca. *Gianni Celati: The Craft of Everyday Storytelling*. Toronto: The University of Toronto Press, 2000.

White, Hayden. *Metahistory: The Historical Imagination in Nineteenth-Century Europe*. Baltimore: The Johns Hopkins University Press, 1973

Povero Kerouac:
Il mito dell'America anni '60 in Italia.
Cesari Fiumi e *La Strada è di tutti*

Silvia Boero

UNIVERSITY OF NORTH CAROLINA, CHAPEL HILL

> Get your motor running
> Get it on the highway
> Looking for adventure
> And whatever comes our way
> (*Born to Be Wild*, Steppenwolf, 1969)

O n the Road di Jack Kerouac, è stato, per almeno tre generazioni d'italiani, un agnostico breviario, un testo di meditazioni, un libro rivelatore, e forse anche uno di ricette di vita. La nostrana beat generation viveva gli anni '60 cercando di seguire le orme di Sal e Dean, e di tutti gli altri strampalati personaggi: certo, non si poteva fare coast to coast, ma non erano pochi quelli che decidevano di attraversare lo stivale, imitando lo stile di vita da strada: una corsa forse meno romantica, ma pur sempre avvincente, considerata l'Italia dell'epoca. Tradotto da Magda De Cristoforo con una prefazione di Fernanda Pivano, *On the Road* usciva in Italia per i tipi della Mondadori, collana Medusa, nel 1959, con il titolo *Sulla Strada*. La sua vera e propria scoperta, però, sarebbe avvenuta con il '68, la cui generazione amò e criticò al tempo stesso il povero Kerouac. Ma perchè povero? In realtà l'Italia è uno dei paesi europei in cui Kerouac gode – ed ha sempre goduto – di ottima fama e reputazione. Un noto quotidiano – La Repubblica – ha offerto *Sulla Strada* nella propria biblioteca nell'aprile di quest'anno, e la beat generation figura come soggetto di studio nei programmi di lingua inglese delle scuole superiori. Dunque, nonostante le critiche, inevitabili per chiunque, Kerouac in Italia è pur sempre uno dei più amati eroi stellestricie, ma "povero" sembra restare a casa sua, nonostante la recente, ma timida, riscoperta da parte della critica statunitense.

Quando, nel 1957, *On the Road* uscì negli Stati Uniti ricevette un'accoglienza ambivalente. Gilbert Millstein, che al tempo si occupava di recensioni per il *New York Times*, lo definì: "a major novel, an authentic work of art, whose appearance is a historic occasion. The writing displays at times a beauty almost breathtaking." Pochi giorni dopo il commento di Millstein, apparve una recensione di David Dempsey sul Times, nell'edizione domenicale. Dempsey definiva *On the Road* "readable and entertaining" ma trovava che "the freaks may be fascinating, but they are hardly part of our lives." Inoltre Kerouac pareva troppo in sintonia con le situazioni altamente immorali di cui trattava: "He could maintain a morally neutral point of view, while recounting incidents of blatant immorality" fu la sentenza, opinione del resto condivisa da Herbert Gold, *The Nation*, il quale forse andò un po' oltre, affermando addirittura che *On the Road* era "a proof of illness rather than creation of art." Truman Capote arrivò a definire "not writing at all, but just typing" la scrittura di Kerouac. Simili recensioni e commenti, contribuirono tuttavia a stabilizzare la sua fama, anche se non in modo conforme alle sue aspettative. Autore colto, era ben cosciente di saper scrivere, e probabilmente non prevedeva una tale inabilità a comprendere da parte della critica. Ma il tempo fu dalla sua parte: *On The Road* pose le basi per un nuovo – almeno in parte – stile di vita.

DIARIO DI VIAGGIO: REALTÀ, FINZIONE, O TUTT'E DUE?

Cesare Fiumi, corrispondente dagli Stati Uniti per il Corriere della Sera, si ripropone nel 1998 con *La Strada è di tutti* di ripercorrere le orme di Kerouac ma senza droga, ne' alcool, tantomeno con lo stesso ritmo da orologio a pendolo. Fiumi è lineare nella narrazione, e sincero. Forse anche Kerouac/Sal era veritiero, ma, si sa, con una pasticca di benzidrina e caricati a whiskey o altro, di viaggi se ne fanno tanti, non necessariamente sulla strada e/o sulla carta geografica e da scrivere. E poi, del resto, chi tra i grandi viaggiatori ha mai veramente detto la verità? Dalla pia Egeria con la sua *Peregrinatio* in Terra Santa, a Bruce Chatwin, bugiardo professionista – ma che fantastico bugiardo! – come facciamo a stabilire la veridicità di un resoconto di viaggi? E' l'eterno dilemma Truth versus Fiction... Paul Theroux, autentico e veritiero viaggiatore, autore di *Patagonia Express*, va in Patagonia in treno, ma il suo *recit*, benchè avvincente, non riesce a coinvolgere come quello del britannico menzognero, suo amico, recentemente sbugiardato da Nicholas Shakespeare.

Fiumi sembra essere proprio sincero, e non solo, ma intrattiene, pure! Vuole toccare, in doveroso pellegrinaggio, tutti i luoghi raggiunti da Sal e Dean. E così non possiamo fare a meno di metterci in viaggio anche noi che leggiamo, magari con una carta geografica alla mano. Ma quale carta? Una di quelle anni '40 che Jack/Sal usava, dopo averla studiata per mesi, dove le highways non c'erano ancora, e che Fiumi stesso si procura? E qui sorge un altro dilemma: come osserva il professor Monga della Vanderbilt University, anche una carta geografica è, in un certo qual modo, menzognera, poichè riproduce in scala, non è speculare, non presenta la realtà com'è; Borges suggeriva paradossalmente che le carte geografiche dovessero essere su scala uno a uno, per ottenere l'autenticità nel persorso del viaggio. Ma di quale viaggio parliamo? Quello fisico, fatto con un qualunque mezzo di trasporto, o quello nella mente, sobria o meno, o quello sulla carta da scrivere? Un racconto – di qualsiasi cosa tratti – è anche un viaggio, che non significa solo partire. Il viaggio è soprattutto acquisire, lasciare, divenire qualcuno e qualcosa. E` un mutamento. Jack va avanti ed indietro, quattro volte, pendolare degli States alla ricerca ed in compagnia di Dean/Neal, diventando ogni volta un altro, facendo del viaggio l'unica dimensione vitale. Ma lo capirà solo a metà libro/viaggio, quando descrive il ritorno di Dean, il giorno di Natale 1948: "A weary young fellow, muscular and ragged, in a T-shirt, unshaven, red-eyed, came to the porch and rang the bell. I opened the door and suddenly realized it was Dean." Sal, dopo una breve conversazione con il proprio alter ego, comprende, una volta tornato nella casa dei parenti, che è ora di ripartire. "I saw the Christmas tree, the presents, and smelled the roasted turkey, and listened to the talk of the relatives, but now the bug was on me again, and the bug's name was Dean Moriarty and I was off another spurt on the road." Qui inizia il vero e proprio Go West! di Sal/Jack. Si fermerà solo quando anche Dean/Neal deciderà di fermarsi, e qui finisce il libro.

Quello che è importante è cosa e quanto il viaggio ha costruito dentro a chi l'ha fatto/ scritto e a chi lo ha letto/fatto. L'attendibilità, intesa come l'aver materialmente visto, udito e toccato, resta un fatto marginale.

IL "VERO" RACCONTO DEL VIAGGIO ALLA RICERCA DEI LUOGHI DEI SOGNI

Per Fiumi la situazione è ben diversa: lui è un giornalista, dunque votato – almeno in teoria – all'obiettività. Ma è impossibile, se non inacettabile, essere obiettivi quando si sogna, o quando si vive dentro una fabbrica di sogni, quali sono gli States. Jack, dunque, è la guida geografico-storico-spirituale migliore che Fiumi potesse trovare. "Avevo appena compiuto quarant'anni. Gli stessi di *On the Road*" ci racconta nell'incipit del libro. Siamo nel '98, quasi trenta sono gli anni trascorsi dalla morte di Jack Kerouac, e Trieste gli dedica, l'anno dopo, una mostra-conferenza, proprio il giorno del suo anniversario. A casa nostra *On the road* continua a far sognare.

La strada è di tutti sembra non porsi l'enigma della veridicità; invece, lungo un itinerario di sedicimila chilometri, delinea magistralmente anche un bel pezzo di storia statunitense, filtrata attraverso gli occhi di un European/Italian to the bone, che però è inguaribilmente attratto dagli States. Talvolta Fiumi si lascia andare ad un tono elegiaco sofferto in onore della morte di una generazione che ha creato un periodo storico-culturale. Allen Ginsberg, il Carlo Marx di *On the Road*, muore nell'aprile '98: quando Fiumi arriva a Pittsburgh pochi giorni dopo, legge, su un quotidiano locale, un articolo dell'opinionista George Will (Fiumi fa i nomi ed anche i cognomi, e fornisce pure le date, forse qui sta la sua veridicità) che denigra il poeta della beat generation facendo allusioni becere alla sua omosessualità, definendolo "solo un volgare esibizionista"; ma, peggio, c'è chi non ne ha mai sentito il nome. Eppure, pochi giorni prima, a Paterson, New Jersey, che diede i natali non solo alle peregrinazioni di Kerouac, ma soprattutto a Ginsberg, la bandiera del municipio era a mezz'asta, in segno di lutto per la sua dipartita decorosa, in sordina. Nel bel mezzo delle solite contraddizioni che caratterizzano gli States, Fiumi pensa con un sorriso che, nemmeno a farlo apposta, la Thunderbird, o Uccello di Tuono, su cui si ripropone di fare il coast to coast fine anni '90 è proprio verde, come quella dei versi di Ginsberg: "Se avessi un'automobile verde/ andrei a trovare il mio vecchio compagno/ nella sua casa sul mare del West" nella poesia dedicata a Neal Cassady, l'amato Dean di Sal Paradise.

Ma il viaggio deve continuare, e bisogna arrivare a Chicago, e andare a dormire proprio all'YMCA, dove anche Sal/Jack aveva pernottato cinquant'anni prima, impaziente di raggiungere Denver e Dean. Cesare attacca discorso con una ragazza in un bar; tra il perplesso e l'annoiato legge il Kerouac di *Mexico City Blues* solo perchè un'amica le ha detto di farlo, ed ora, arrivata a metà, gli confessa di non sapere davvero cosa pensarne. Il povero Kerouac non parla più alla sua America, o forse non era mai nemmeno riuscito a sussurrarle nell'orecchio. Pare davvero che quest'America fine anni '90, in fase clintoniana discendente, dopo aver accettato supinamente il reganismo, voglia dimenticare tutto ciò che di esaltante ed ispiratore aveva avuto per diverse generazioni locali, ma soprattutto europee ed italiane.

Fiumi si ferma a bighellonare un pochino nel centro di Chicago, per finire, quasi guidato dal vate dell'auto verde in un "one dollar store." Vale la pena di riportare per intero il dialogo tra l'autore/viaggiatore (vogliamo chiamarlo pellegrino?) e la commessa, di nome Evelyn e le conseguenti osservazioni. E. "Da dove viene? Che strada ha fatto per venire a Chicago?" C. "Sono passato dalla Pennsylvania" E. "Ci sono i dollari in Pensylvania?" C. "Come, scusi?" E. "Si paga con i dollari anche in Pennsylvania?"

C. "Credo che da voi negli States si paghi con i dollari ovunque..." E. "Lei non è degli Stati Uniti?" C. "No, vengo dall'Italia" E. "E che lingua si parla in Italia?"

C. "l'Italiano..." E. "Italiano? Davvero?" Evelyn sorrise ad una simile notizia, ed evitò di chiedere se da noi si pagasse in dollar. Soltanto qualche giorno più tardi, quando un'altra signora mi chiese se in Italia avevamo il telefono, capii cosa intendeva Kerouac per la grande omologazione americana: quell'analfabetismo di ritorno in cui va a morire anche la libertà, l'idea terribile, molto americana, di chi pensa di riassumere in sè tutto il mondo, negando persino esistenze diverse. Non in una fattoria sperduta dell'Idaho, ma al banco di un negozio di North Clark, nel caos multietnico di Chicago.".

Oltrepassate le campagne dell'Illinois, Fiumi, nella sua nostalgica ricerca dei luoghi visitati da Jack/Sal e

Neal/Dean, scopre che altri americani sono passati di lí. Anche Jack London, clandestino sui treni, che probabilmente avrà ispirato Jack/Sal nel suo viaggio da *hobo*, un capolavoro romantico: "The greatest ride of my life was about to come up, a truck, with a flatboard at the back, with about six or seven boys sprawled out on it, and the drivers, two young blond farmers from Minnesota, were picking up every single soul they found on that road." Questa volta Jack è hobo, non sul treno, ma su un autocarro divenuto, per bontà dei proprietari, microcosmo degli hobos dell'asfalto. Sal è accolto bene dalla piccola comunità vagabonda e subito gli passano una bottiglia: "I took a swig in the wild, lyrical, drizzling air of Nebraska." Sal/Jack – colui che cerca, l'eroe in viaggio, vuole ubriacarsi non solo di alcool, ma anche di avventure, e ne inventa di magnifiche.

Cesare, invece, per niente hobo, ma piuttosto paladino dell'italica stirpe anni '60-'70 che ha sognato a ritmo di rock'n'roll le strade di Jack, spera non tanto di inventare storie, ma di ritrovare qualcosa che è Storia, con la maiuscola: quell'America cantata da Kerouac, che – il nostrano pellegrino comincia ad capirlo – non c'è mai stata. Forse Jack, franco-canadese-americano, sperava, per bocca dell'italo-americano Sal Paradise di rendere veri i suoi sogni, ma qualche ingrediente mancava nella formula. Fiumi, con sua sorpresa, scopre un'altra America, che forse vale ancor di più di quella immaginata e sperata da Kerouac e dalle genarazioni di beatnicks in tutto il mondo. E` un'America che non vuole dimenticare. Nell'ancora ghiacciato Michigan primaverile, ad Ann Arbor, qualcuno vuole tenere viva – ed ad ogni costo, addirittura con un piccolo museo – la memoria del grande Jesse Owens, che alle Olimpiadi di Berlino del '36 stracciò tutti i record di atletica, facendo schiattare di rabbia – purtroppo non del tutto – il Fuhrer.

Quasi dietro l'angolo del Midwest, proprio sulla soglia del vero e proprio West, a Winterset, Iowa, Cesare scopre la casa di John Wayne – e ci trova pure un museo a lui dedicato, ma patetico come il *Gion Vaine* "italiaco", lo Zeus di quell'Olimpo cinematografico americano...made in Italy: "Andai a vedere la casa natale di John Wayne. Quattro stanze in tutto, un po' di ricordi e qualche memorabilia:

locandine e documenti. Jan, la direttrice della casa-museo, fu molto disponibile e mi mostró il libro degli ospiti ed un suo archivio statistico: ogni anno almeno quindici italiani passavano di lí." Con ritmo ineguale, ma costante nelle emozioni, Fiumi passa dall'Iowa al Nebraska, dove lo colgono le visioni suggerite dalla lettura di Willa Cather, che forse si trovava proprio là, in quelle stesse pianure dove la desolazione è la sola compagnia, quando cominciò a scrivere *My Antonia*. Finalmente è a Denver "lungo la strada madre del libro, nella direzione dei desideri" ma Jack, quando aveva appena toccato la *mile high city*, già sognava "Frisco": "Suddenly we came down from a mountain and overlooked the great sea-plain of Denver. I was hitching to get on to S. Francisco." L'arrivo in California, dopo Salt Lake City ed il Nevada, è annunciato non tanto dal cielo blu e dall'aria balsamica già ben visualizzata dalla penna di Kerouac, ma dal fatto di *sentirefrisco* come la sentiva Jack/Sal, che lì trascorse i suoi giorni da guardiano insieme all'amico Remi Boncoeur, l'esatto opposto di Dean, ma che per un po' gli contese il posto nel cuore di Sal.

Si termina con la deviazione a sud, in Arizona e Texas, dove Fiumi spera di incontrare il novello Kerouac – almeno secondo lui e parte della critica italiana – Cormac McCarthy. Non solo perchè hanno in comune la strada nel senso letterale del termine, ma perchè entrambi "viaggiano" nel cuore dell'America che spesso l'establishment politico di turno vuole nascondere, ma che tanto acchiappa chi americano non lo è.

Jack, *on the road* nel Texas, nell'ultimo viaggio si dirige verso il Messico, mitico luogo dove poter raggiungere la libertà dalle convenzioni, ma anche miniera da sfruttare per moltissimi gringos: "It's the world, said Dean, My God, he cried slapping the wheel, It's the world, think of it. Sonofabitch! Gowddamn!" Come giustamente ha osservato Robert Holton della Okanagan University College, "Mexico represents the way out of the "white ambitions" that Sal has been seeking; he and Dean feel utterly elated at the sense of possibility that opens up for them once they leave the United States."

Siamo quasi alla fine: l'italico pellegrino si dirige verso Los Angeles, da dove ripartirà per l'Italia. E' ancora notte, ma fra poco sorgerà il sole. E Fiumi, ormai dentro fino al collo nel mito beat, esprime l'ultimo desiderio del suo viaggio nei sogni di una generazione statunitense e di almeno tre italiane: "Se dovevo veder sorgere il sole da una strada – il mio ultimo sole di viaggiatore – che almeno fosse una strada bianca e polverosa. Poi avrei raggiunto Los Angeles, a mi sarei congedato da Uccello di Tuono." Non abbiamo nessun Dean da cui congedarsi in una fredda sera del New Jersey, ne' vediamo Fiumi "sballare" per un tramonto o per una bella chicana (o, almeno, lui non ce lo fa sapere)

Accuratissimo nei riferimenti di carattere storico-letterario-musicale (il rock'nroll é sempre presente, nel mangianastri dell'auto verde e nel testo) Fiumi non si pone in *La strada é di Tutti* problematiche di natura critica. Non parla delle tecniche di scrittura tipiche di Kerouac, anche se cita il manuale che scrisse; fa accenni all'invidia di Capote, ma l'analisi della "lingua" di Kerouac non c'è, e nemmeno ci dovrebbe essere in questo libro, che altro non è che un omaggio quasi funebre. Non fa notare la quasi inesistenza delle donne nell'opera di Kerouac: sì, esistono, ma solo perchè sono *beautiful babes* con cui trascorrere allegramente un po' di tempo, anche quando vengono sposate. Jack/Sal, del resto, amò la moglie di Neal/Dean, forse perchè così poteva amare anche lui un po' di più. Nemmeno Fiumi si sofferma sulla presunta omossessualità latente in *On theRoad*, che, se c'è, ci sta anche bene, calza a pennello a questa *brotherhood of males*. L'autore però sottolinea l'origine non anglosassone dello scrittore e del protagonista, entrambi provenienti da famiglie di immigrati, ma che della terra d'origine hanno dimenticato molto, e non la vanno a cercare – come fece invece Ferlinghetti, altro genio beat, nelle sue peregrinazioni italiane. Jack/Sal non sa ancora cosa siano gli States e come siano fatti, scoprirli è la sua priorità. Per Fiumi, oltre all'elegia, l'altro scopo è rivisitare l'eterno leit motiv del "hero on a journey" in tutti i suoi aspetti, ed all'introspezione Fiumi riesce ad unire felicemente il carattere divulgativo. La sua prosa è fluida come quella degli interminabili nastri d'asfalto statunitensi; garbata anche quando fustiga, è divertente e profonda. La *Strada è di tutti* è la resa dei conti con una cultura che non ci è mai appartenuta, ma che abbiamo voluto fare nostra a tutti i costi. E' un omaggio all'-

ultima storia western che non è mai stata portata sul grande schermo. E' il risveglio da un lungo sogno, ma giusto in tempo per potersi riaddormentare e sognare ancora di più e meglio lo stesso sogno. E' quello che tanti Italiani avrebbero voluto essere, liberi anche loro come Sal e Dean dalle convenzioni dettate da due società in sfacelo – la nostra e la loro degli anni '50, con i rispettivi dopoguerra: il nostro affrontato nel tentativo di contestualizzarlo storicamente, il loro seppellito sotto la finta spensieratezza, maschera d'obbligo da indossarsi – sotto la cupa egida del maccartismo – per esorcizzare il maniacale timore della guerra fredda. Kerouac nel dopoguerra rappresentò – a casa sua – la tipica ventata d'aria fresca, ma che al tempo stesso confermava la presenza dell'odore stantio di una *grand narrative* ormai andata a male. Jack stesso andava alla scoperta dell'America, di mondo diverso e possibile, del quale sia lui che noi dall'altra parte del mondo sapevamo poco, ma in cui avevamo tanta fiducia. In un collettivo Go West! siamo tutti partiti, per arrivare a scoprire che il viaggio può essere eterno. Sí, è vero, la terra finisce, la grande terra d'America, i cui cantori ci hanno sempre coinvolti, noi, europei smagati e vecchi, anche quando avevamo vent'anni o di meno. Ma, ad un certo punto alla fine della terra, del viaggio e del libro – tutti insieme perchè sono tutti la stessa cosa – comincia il travaglio del mare dei quesiti che ogni viaggiatore si pone: perchè si è viaggiato, cosa ci ha dato e tolto, e dove veramente siamo stati dentro di noi. Si riparte, allora con il ritorno, per dirla con il Ricardo Reis di Saramago, da quello stesso punto dove siamo arrivati, "aqui onde o mar se acabou e a terra espera."

OPERE CONSULTATE

Challis, C. *Quest for Kerouac*. Boston: Faber & Faber, 1984.
Fiumi, C. *La Strada è di Tutti*. Milano: Feltrinelli, 1997.
Robert, H. *On the Road: Kerouac's Ragged American Journey*. New York: Twayne, 1999.
Kerouac, J. *On the Road*. New York: Viking, 1957.
Saramago, J. *O Ano da Morte de Ricardo Reis*. Lisboa: Caminho, 1984.

Surprising Origins in Italian Horror:
Florentine 18th century Wax Anatomical Models

Annette Burfoot
QUEEN'S UNIVERSITY

The literature surrounding the study of the horror film genre is well established. The 1980s witnessed a remarkable consideration of horror from the point of view of the psychoanalyst, with feminist critics present from the start. Out of the French, particularly feminist philosophies of the 1960s and 1970s (Kristeva, 1982; Irigaray, 1985), came the crucial links between Freudian dramas between mother, fathers, daughters and sons, and the representation of the abject (Mulvey, 1981; Kaplan, 1983; Modleski, 1986; Butler, 1990; Clover, 1992; Creed, 1993). Of course, there is also considerable attention in literature to the gothic novel and the horror tale (many horror films are the book-to-film translations of these novels such as *Frankenstein, Dracula* and so on) Yet, there remains an unappreciated source of the principles of modern horror: early modern scientific representations of the body. An incredible example of these can be found in the 18th century museum of the natural and physical sciences in Florence, Italy. This extensive collection of life-size and very life-like wax models in various states of dissection can be seen as the earliest "cinematic" representations of the body as the liminal subject between fear and rationality; key components of the horror genre.

This paper interrogates these scientific models in terms of principles of horror. The terms of reference are drawn from the psychoanalytic perspective (chiefly Creed and Clover) that, in turn, addresses the Freudian primal scene and masculine transference in finding a way "out" of the horrific. The terms shall also include a socio-cultural analysis based on the work of Martin Tropp (1990), who argues the significance of a historical cultural analysis of horror myths as formative to the modern social imaginary.

PRINCIPLES OF HORROR

Two key contributors to and popularizers of the feminist study of the horror film genre are undoubtedly Carol Clover with *Men Women and Chainsaws* (1992), and Barbara Creed with *The Monstrous Feminine* (1993). Creed and Clover develop an accessible and convincing critique of horror as masculine catharsis of fundamental fears. I will focus on Creed's use of the primal scene in analyzing horror as feminine abjection and Clover's "final girl" as a masculine strategy in the face of monstrous threat.

Creed distinguishes between pre-oedipal and archaic mothers; the first representing a maternal presence restricted within a phallic economy as undistinguished from the child and therefore not yet a contested possession as in the oedipal stage. The archaic mother is how Creed attempts to rescue the "mythological figure of woman as the source of all life" with a self-referential womb from a negative reconstruction that is "the dread of the generative mother seen only in the abyss, the monstrous vagina, the origin of all life threatening to reabsorb what it once birthed" (1990; p. 135). Creed illustrates the activation of this principle in horror with an in depth analysis of the horror/science fiction classic, *Alien* (1979). She describes the main monster, the alien, and what it does with human bodies in terms of the abject-as-corpse (embodying the putrid); the abject-as-boundary transgressor (ruptures and colonizes bodies), and the abject-as-maternal (tubular hells and killer births).

Clover analyzes exploitation, slasher horror films of the 1970s and 1980s (*Texas Chain Saw Massacre, Halloween* and so on). She pays particular attention to the role of the "Final Girl" or the usually virginal young woman who remains to fell the killer after a period of slaughter of sacrificial lambs, one-by-one, by a crazed and monstrous man/monster. Clover argues that this last girl, untouched heterosexually and thus open to sexual transformation in a heterosexist ideology, represents the male psyche and masculine frailties in the face of profound and horrible threat. S/he is the one who restores order and containment after bodies have been mutilated and turned inside out by chainsaws, blades and so on.

Lastly, I want to turn to a much lesser known con-
tributor to the literature on horror, Martin Tropp and his
work in *Images of Fear* (1990). Tropp's approach does not
take the psychoanalytic route but the social, particularly a
form of historical cultural study. Because he engages with
the origins of the horror story (Gothic romance), he con-
centrates on novels rather than film. He compares the
three main horror stories of the 19th century, *Frankenstein, Dracula* and *The Strange Case of Dr. Jekyll and Mr.
Hyde*, with significant socio-cultural events in the late
1800s and early 1900s: the industrial revolution and
mechanization, the liberation of women and the working
class, urbanization, and the first World War. Tropp's is an
innovative and convincing demonstration of how "these
materials [...] connect individual lives with the group experience of culture; horror in fiction moved from a safe re-
moteness to a frightening immediacy, from subjective to
objective reality" (5). He points to the 19th century factory-
castles sprouting up throughout Europe, home to both
great mechanical beasts built on social promise and the
horrors of child labor and other class exploitation. The image of Frankenstein's monster was used in social demon-
strations to symbolize the body politic gone horribly
wrong, while Tropp displays the links between the Dr.
Jekyll story and the Jack-the-Ripper murders as evidence
of growing anxieties over class boundaries (both Dr. Jekyll
and Jack are thought to be men of a cultured class who
secretly sport wild and savage behavior, especially towards
lower-class women). Finally, the eroticism in the story of
Dracula is characterized as the bringing of women "to a
frightening new power" in light of women's social and political emancipation (139).

WAX MODELING

La Specola is considered the oldest public museum in
the western world and is located near and connected via
corridors to the grand former Florentine home of the Tus-
can Dukes, Palazzo Pitti, the Uffizi (where the Ducal
treasures were housed) and Palazzo Vecchio (the seat of
the Duchy's government). It was inaugurated in 1775 as
the Imperiale Regio Museo di Fisica e Storia Naturale (The
Imperial Royal Museum of Physics and Natural History)

and from its inception was open to all classes of the public. The site not only provided a passive and public science education, it also became an institute of formal study and experimentation. Several years before its inauguration, La Specola (as it became commonly known once its Osservatorio Astronomica was added in 1780) housed a ceroplastic studio (where wax anatomical models were made). In about 1790, scientific subjects began to be taught at the site and a science library was established. In 1923 it became the University of Florence and the museum now contains the University's Department of Physics and Natural Sciences. Today only the zoological collection and anatomical ceroplastics remain at the original museum site (physics and astronomy were moved in 1869 to the nearby hill of Arcetri where Galileo spent his last years).

The use of wax models for the study of the body can be dated back to the medieval age and Alessandra Giliani of Persiceto (d. 1326) who was a Bolognese prosector (an assistant to anatomists and surgeons whose business it was to dissect dead bodies in preparation for anatomical research or demonstration). However, wax modeling was not reserved to the emerging professions of medicine and modern science. Leonardo da Vinci and Michelangelo both created wax anatomical models of life-sized and "flayed" bodies (the skin is removed to reveal underlying muscle formations etc.). This was a common activity for renaissance artists in their pursuit of passionately and realistically rendering the human body in stone and paint.

The collection of wax anatomical models at La Specola number in the hundreds and include over a dozen full-scale models in various stages of dissection. The models are distributed throughout eight rooms and are in their original display cases and in their original positions. The display is designed to start with the more superficial and gross (in terms of gross anatomy) aspects of the body (stance and structure based on skeletal and muscular aspects) to the more mysterious and functional aspects of the body (nerves, the endocrine system, internal organs, and reproduction). All models are made of wax and some have additions of hair and eyelashes to heighten the realistic effect. The models (both full body and parts) are accompanied by framed pictures of the model surrounded by radiating lines pointing to numbers that correspond to a typography of parts and function kept in small drawers under the glass cases. One of the models, a gynaecological life-sized model, has removable parts. The museum was designed as a visual and interactive medical and science teaching aid.

The proximity of this museum-cum-classroom to the ducal residence, seat of power and the prestigious art collections signifies a growing social significance for the empirical sciences. Galileo's struggle with the papacy and eventual triumph over church dogma is beautifully illustrated in an alter-like setting, La Tribuna di Galileo, also housed in the same building as La Specola. Here we find visual testimony to his triumphant gaze in the form of his telescopic eye in a fresco depicting his presentation of a telescope and his account of the moons of Jupiter to the papal court. It is no coincidence that set in the center of this chapel-like tribute is a stature of Galileo with no reference to divine intervention. Scientific rationality has replaced Christian dogma as authoritative knowledge.

FEMINIST SOCIO-CULTURAL ANALYSIS OF ANATOMY-AS-HORROR

Unfortunately it is very difficult today for the public to access this tribute to Galileo, unlike the collection of zoological models, including the anatomical waxes housed one story above, which are not only open to the public but are the focus for regular school trips. This part of La Specola has always been open to the public, and to all classes of the public (as long as they were clean and presentable). As such, this museum in particular, but also the emerging visual culture of modern science in general, opened up the new empirical world to venues beyond the traditional closed doors of its courtly and priestly patrons. Following the practice of dramatic display of dissection (they were performed in semi-public "theatres"), these models formed a contemporary popular culture.[1] And one

---

[1] This spectacle has been recently revived within the notorious German plastination exhibit, *Body Worlds*, which features actual cadavers that have been impregnated with a plastic resin, dissected and mounted in various positions (for example, running and riding a horse) and in

of the main draws of the display was the exciting journey into the mysterious terrain of the body's interior, with the most exciting scene of all in the gynecological room. This is the spectacle of horror that we will now examine.

The eight anatomical rooms are designed to be walked thorough in a certain order: from the outward and visual manifestations of the human body (muscles and skeleton) to the inside and functional aspects (circulatory and nervous systems, organs, and reproduction). Besides establishing a persistent distinction between form and function in modern medicine, this distinction draws significantly on dualistic gendered assumptions regarding life and death, rationality and carnality, fear and desire. Remarkably, it also presages Freud and Lacan's interpretation of the primal scene that underlies so much interpretation of the horror scene as psychic catharsis.

Almost everyone walking into the first room of models (skeletal and muscle systems) recoils at the hyper-realism of the skinned models that surround and fill the room. Skulls perch atop rather elegant figures that assume upright and animated postures. Other figures lounge horizontally in large glass cabinets; skinned faces resting on bony and sinewy hands and arms (see Fig. 1). The carefully crafted and colored wax reveals every anatomical detail and provides a constant reminder of how time will treat our bodies the same way as death and decay will strip our mortality, layer by layer, to the bare bones.

But these models, the skeleton-as-gentleman, are replaced by more horrific dissections that follow. Ironically these later models have "more to them" in the sense that they display the circulatory, nerve and endocrine systems so that one sees the skeletal and muscular base covered with veins and arteries, glands and nerves. Although this additional anatomical detail and more precise dissection

---

various states of dissection (one flayed model stands holding its skin like a lumpy cloak). See Gunther Von Hagens and Angelina Whalley (2000). The plastination innovator and director of the plastination exhibit, Gunther von Hagens, has recently drawn fire in Britain for performing public dissections for a fee.

draws us nearer to the moment of violation or the cutting into the body, these figures remain more mechanistic than organismic. Thus what could be horrific, skinned human bodies, appears almost comical. In contrast, a sense of edging towards the abyss is heightened as you move into the next room where three female models lie prostrate in their respective glass cases. Up to now, no full figure has much in the way of skin or hair and, as such, seem unbelievable as humans and more like some form of organic robot or cyborg. Inversely the female figures have plenty of signs of what we hold to be human. Designed to exhibit the internal organs and the digestive system, the models of the young beautiful women with long plaited hair lie with their torsos cut from clavicle to pubis and the innards pulled out and draped over both sides of nubile torsos. Their heads are tilted backwards exposing the neck and inviting the viewer in as if in a scene that crosses between Dracula and Jack the Ripper. The female models' faces are masks of a sort of drugged rapture, their lips partially open and their beautiful but unfocused eyes gazing into the distance. Their hands are gracefully poised by their sides, with one of the figures holding her own plait (see Fig. 2).

This visual feast of gore and the erotic continues. Down the corridor from this large room is a much smaller room on the way out of the museum (resonating with the Bataillian notion of the dreaded lower half of the body as fecal exit, among other things, Battaille; 1962). It is the gynecological room containing Clemente Susini's "decomposable" or modular female figure: "the doll" (Fig. 3). This is a hands-on model that is designed to have the front panel of the torso removed to reveal four successive levels of dissection. The deepest level includes an opened uterus with a five-month fetus inside. The model in its closed form is remarkably worked in terms of rendering a beautiful and erotic female figure. The likeness is of a young woman, again supine with her head tilted back and slightly to one side as if in some state of sexual ecstasy. Her young firm breasts sport erect nipples, her lips are slightly parted and she stares dreamily off into the distance. One leg is slightly bent allowing us to look directly at her external genitals (rendered complete with pubic hair). This model is normally displayed closed.

This "medical venus" is surrounded by full-sized models of the female uterus (heavily pregnant in most cases) with the women's large amputated thigh stumps framing the external genitalia and the dissected womb (see Fig. 4). Skin, fat and muscle are peeled back like a huge orange to reveal either a distended pregnant uterus or a well-developed fetus or fetuses inside. There are also cabinets containing a large collection of fetuses in all stages of gestation (although the earlier models illustrate homonculism – fully formed miniature humans – rather than embryology as it is understood today). There are also a choir of dissected newborns, almost all male and positioned in a baby Christ-like pose with little arms reaching outwards to embrace and bless, and a slightly tilted head gazing down knowingly and forgivingly on the observer and the doll (see Fig. 5). Within this womb-like, small and packed room, any mystery of anatomical femininity is exposed – there are no surprises left and the mystery of life itself softly glows in waxy realism that both shocks and delights. And off in a corner of the gynecological room is a beribboned phallus – a large penis separate from any other part of the male genitalia with a little bow wrapped around its base. It lies at the foot of the doll, near her genitalia and serves as a phallic pointer within a patriarchal display of curiosity and fetish.

The "little venus," also by Susini, is at the Museum of the Poggi Palace in Bologna. With La Specola's doll, these two decomposable (as translated literally from the Italian "scomponibile") figures are female, young and typically beautiful, and form elegant and erotic presents or packages. Laura Mulvey analyzes the metaphoric implications of Pandora's box in terms of Pandora-AS-box. She describes Pandora, along the lines of Creed's all-defining archaic mother, as the "mythic origin of surface/secret and interior/exterior topography" (55). Mulvey uses the myth to illustrate feminine-as-fetish (the psychoanalytical reaction to profound and primordial fears) and draws parallels to Trojan horses, the Christian myth of woman as the origin of betrayal and knowledge, as well as to modern robots and cyborgs (which are often beautifully feminine and bear dangerous knowledge as technology-gone-amok). The 18th-century female wax figures of La Specola deserve to be included in the list. Their exterior exquisite beauty-as-feminine draws the eye into the terrifying interior of liter-ally spilled guts. The mysterious lack, the womb, and the entrance to the vagina, are all laid out for rational com-prehension and celebration over dark, dangerous, chaotic nature. These models are the Final Girl of the material (disease and early death) as well as the metaphorical (fe-minine as mysterious betrayer and site of origin) horrors of 18th-century Europe. They are embodiments of our fears of body-based fragility and mortality, and they bring these same bodies into the ordered world of modern scientific rationalism.

The social and political contexts of these bodies are also significant. Although it is possible to apply Trope's Victorian icons of horror to contemporary conceptualiza-tions of these figures (women's emancipation, the indus-trial revolution), a brief consideration of the contexts from when they were created reveals a different iconography that plays prominently in the rise of modern scientific ra-tionalism. These models form a logical extension of scien-tific sight associated with Galileo. For as the telescope was developed and disseminated widely throughout Europe and beyond in the 17th century, so was its inverse, the mi-croscope. As eyes turned skyward, so did they enter the body and other unchartered territories decrying dogmatic and mythic representations for the naked-eye truth. And the Grand Duke of Tuscany, Peter Leopold's (1747-1792) decision to collect together the scientific "curiosities" of the Duchy in La Specola, to augment them with increasingly popular anatomical waxes effectively making the museum a working medical school, and to open the display to the public, both heralded the rise of empiricism as a new world order and provided the spectacle of its triumph over the horrific other. Rationalism takes an embodied ana-tomical form logically inscribing and containing the body even as it opens it up. Surfing the edge of this wave of modern scientific ideology is the archaic, monstrous femi-nine, tamed somewhat through the scientific scribing and sexual objectification. Anxieties remain. Alignments of fleshed and desirous features with gore and the feminine as site of origin return us to primal fears of the generational matrix. But as Creed argues, it is important to distinguish prescription from description (1990; p. 140). This display of horrified science makes sense but needn't.

ILLUSTRATIONS

Fig. 1 – Wax Model of Skinned Man

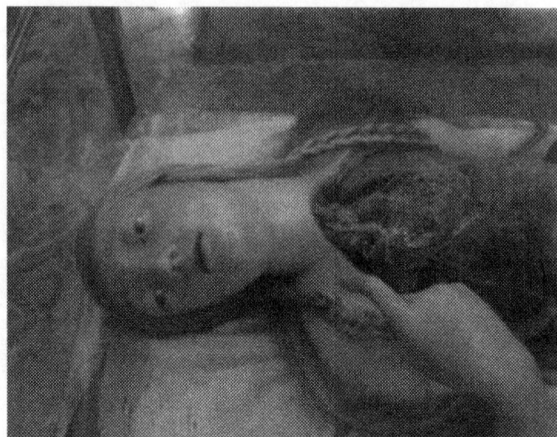

Fig. 2 – Wax Model of Woman with Open Torso

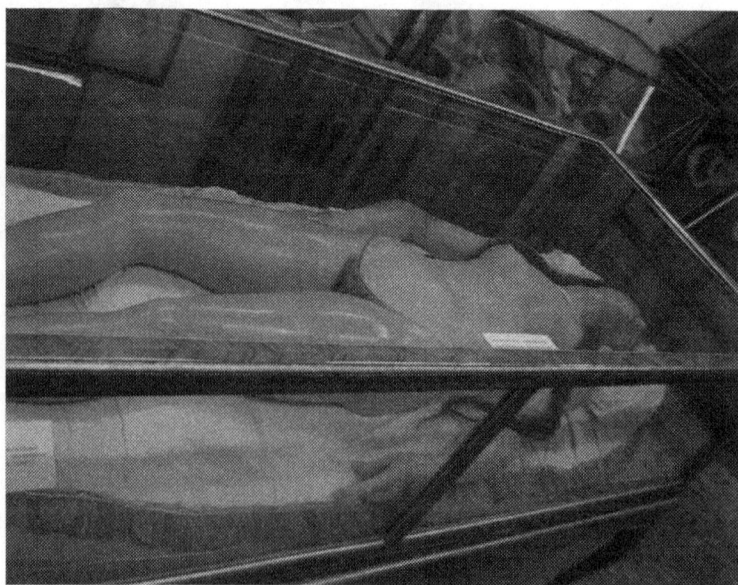

Fig. 3 – The Doll

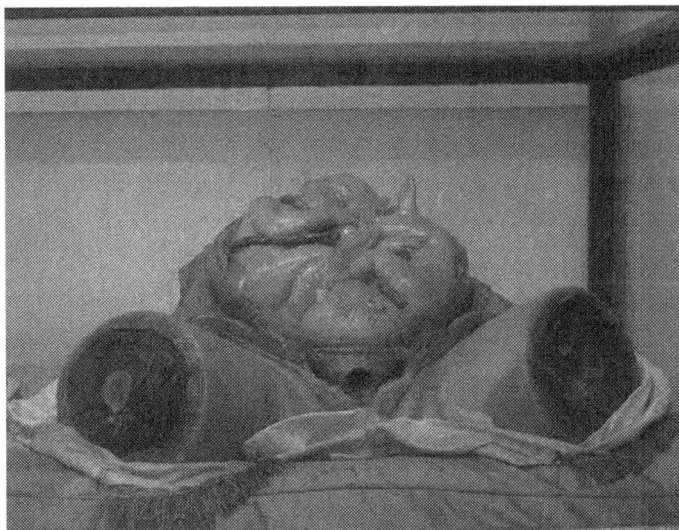

Fig. 4 – Wax Model of Woman's Trunk with Twins

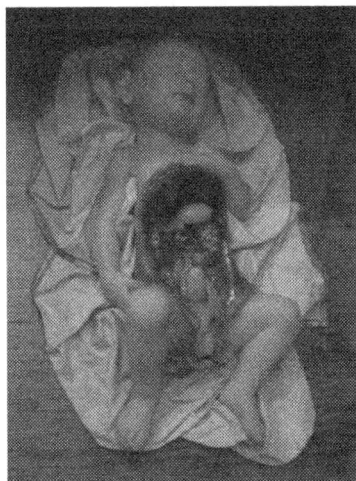

Fig. 5 – Wax Model of Infant

REFERENCES

Bataille, Georges. *Death and Sensuality: A Study of Eroticism and Taboo.* New York: Walker, 1962.

Butler, Judith. "The Force of Fantasy: Feminism, Mapplethorpe, and Discursive Excess," *Differences* 2 (1990): 105-25.

Clover, Carol. *Men, Women and Chainsaws: Gender in the Modern Horror Film.* Princeton: Princeton UP, 1992.

Creed, Barbara. *The Monstrous Feminine: Film, Feminism and Psychoanalysis.* New York: Routledge, 1993.

___. "*Alien* and the Monstrous Feminine." *Alien Zone: Cultural Theory and Contemporary Science Fiction Cinema.* Ed. Annette Kuhn. London: Verso, 1990.

Encyclopædia Anatomica. Köln, Ger.: Taschen, 1999.

Irigaray, Luce. *This Sex Which is Not One.* Trans. Catherine Porter. New York: Cornell UP, 1985.

Kaplan, E. Ann. *Women and Film: Both Sides of the Camera.* London: Methuen, 1983.

Kristeva, Julia. *Powers of Horror: An Essay on Abjection.* Trans. Leon Roudiez. New York: Columbia UP, 1982.

Modleski, Tania. "The Terror of Pleasure: The Contemporary Horror Film and Postmodern Theory." *Studies in Entertainment.* Ed. Tania Modleski. Bloomington: Indiana UP, 1986.

Mulvey, Laura. "Pandora's Box: Topographies of Curiosity." *Fetishism and Curiosity.* Bloomington: Indiana UP, 1996.

___. *Visual and Other Pleasures.* Bloomington: Indiana UP, 1981.

Tropp, Martin. *Images of Fear: How Horror Stories Helped Shape Modern Culture (1818-1918).* Jefferson, NC: McFarland, 1999; 1990.

Von Hagens, Gunther and Angelina Whalley. *Anatomy Art: Fascination Beneath the Surface.* Catalogue. Heidelberg: Institute for Plastination, 2000.

Homesick for the Unknown:
Ulysses (1954) and Postwar Pressures to Re-Domesticate the American Male

Frank Burke
QUEEN'S UNIVERSITY

M ario Camerini's *Ulysses* (*Ulisse* [1954]) is the first major product of "Hollywood on the Tiber," as the Hollywood press dubbed the enormous 1950s intervention of the American film industry in Italian film production in Rome.[1] It was part of a postwar revival of the historico-mythico-religious "serious" epic, hearkening back to the silent era, that had its share of Italian incarnations (*Fabiola* [1948], *La Regina di Saba* [1952], *Spartaco* [1953], *Attila* [1954], and *Beatrice Cenci* [1956]) but was dominated by Hollywood productions such as *Quo Vadis?* and *David and Bathsheba* (1951); *Julius Caesar, The Robe,* and *Salome* (1953); *Demetrius and the Gladiators* and *The Silver Chalice* (1954); *Alexander the Great* and *The Prodigal* (1955); *The Ten Commandments* (1956); *Ben-Hur* (1959); and *Spartacus* (1960).[2] Many of the American epics were shot in Rome, serving as the training ground for Italian film artists and technicians, including Sergio Leone.

The "Hollywood-on-the-Tiber" phenomenon was, of course, part of a much larger reality: the enormous influence of the United States not only economically but ideologically on Italian postwar culture. Stephen Gundle has

---

[1] For discussions on the influence of Hollywood and American culture in Italian filmmaking, see Ellwood, and Brunetta and Wagstaff.

[2] The American epic phenomenon did not end with *Spartacus*, it continued on into the mid-1960s with films such as *Cleopatra* (1963) and, although *Cleopatra* pretty much doomed the genre, *The Fall of the Roman Empire* (1964) and *The Greatest Story Ever Told* (1965).

Ulysses also served as a precursor to the much schlockier "peplum" or sword-and-sandal epic of the later 1950s and early 1960s which, though produced in Italy, starred for the most part American (or British) body builders and owed its auspicious debut to the entrepreneurial efforts of Joseph E. Levine, who made Steve Reeves's *Hercules* (*Le fatiche di Ercole*) hugely profitable in America. This paved the way for nearly 200 *Hercules* spin-offs (though often with different heroes such as Samson, "Ursus," and "Maciste") in a span of little more than five years.

called Italy "the most receptive country in Europe, in the 1950s, to American cultural inputs" (563; trans. Duggan 13). And as Christopher Duggan notes: "few aspects of daily life remained untouched: films, television programmes, glossy magazines, popular music, industrial design, fashion and language (with the introduction of dozens of anglicisms), all bore the heavy imprint of America in this period" (13).

Ulysses is a highly instructive example of the Americanization of Italian cinema in the 1950s. Despite being directed by an Italian and shot in Italy, *Ulysses* was produced by Carlo Ponti and Dino Di Laurentiis in conjunction with an American – William W. Schorr – and with American money. The protagonist is played by Kirk Douglas, and several of the major technical personnel, including the director of photography, were American. Most important, three prominent American screenwriters, Hugh Gray, Ben Hecht, and Irwin Shaw, were involved in writing the story. For all this, plus the its obvious indebtedness to the contemporaneous Hollywood "supercolossal," Gian Piero Brunetta has called *Ulysses* a film "all'Americana" (456). In fact, the cultural issues at stake in *Ulysses* are, arguably, as much or more American than Italian. This might seem unlikely, since numerous aspects of Homer's *Odyssey* (the source for the film) and of *Ulysses* itself resonate with what was then Italy's recent wartime experience: an island (read penisular) society occupied by strangers (the suitors);[3] a virtual state of civil war; a lack of leadership and a consequent void in political authority; and, of course, the desperate need to be liberated. In addition, the archipelagic geography of the *Odyssey*, composed of one isolated setting after another, evokes the *campanilismo* and fragmentation internal to Italy itself, while the hero – *bella figura* and *artista d'arrangiarsi* par excellence – captures perfectly certain aspects of the Italian machismo ideal. Finally, the *Odyssey*, and more pre-

---

[3] Actually, in the poem, the suitors are not all strangers; many are from Ithaca. But in the movie, Penelope asserts "you are all strangers on this island," bringing the film into closer alignment with the Italian wartime occupation experience.

cisely *Ulysses*, are stories of postwar readjustment, of a soldier and his family addressing the former's return to a domestic peacetime environment, certainly an issue for many Italians following the second world war.

However, it is precisely in terms of the last that *Ulysses* seems at times more ideologically American than Italian. For one thing, personal readjustment (as opposed to political, economic, and social reconstruction) was not a major issue in popular consciousness by 1954 in Italy,[4] while in the United States, it persisted throughout much of the 1950s. Secondly, postwar readjustment in the United States – the focus of this essay – was linked to gender in ways that are strikingly reproduced in *Ulysses*. The film addresses the "re-domestication" of men following war, crises in masculinity that derived (largely) from re-domestication, and a consequent "disciplining" of women, reflecting contemporary cultural debates in 1950s America and seeking, as did those debates, to manage male postwar anxiety and (re)secure patriarchy in a society undergoing profound economic and social change.

RE-DOMESTICATION,
GENDER, AND 1950S AMERICA[5]

In *Masked Men: Movies and Masculinities in the 1950s*, Steven Cohan points to a "standard biography common to all adult American men: their experience first as soldiers on the battlefield in World War II (or Korea), then as heads of a middle-class household upon their return" (34). He also notes how this biography gets played out as the need for 1950s America to domesticate man's more "natural" drives and urges (aggression, independence, adventurousness) by turning the soldier into the head-of-the-household, as well as into a "man in a gray flannel suit"[6] (34-35 and passim). This pressure to transform the returning combatant into a *pater familias* was obviously intended to shore up the family as the center of reproduction (both biological and ideological) and of social cohesion. The pressure to create men in gray flannel suits was linked largely to the newfound role of the United States in the wake of World War II as a globally dominant economic power, increasingly conscious of the need not only to maintain but expand its domination. In this context, the "organization man"[7] became a new American hero. The conformity implied by both the "man in the gray flannel suit" and the "organization man" was largely the result of the desire for security produced by the Cold War: the need to be protected in the face of unspeakable threat and the willingness to sacrifice individuality and autonomy in order to feel secure. As Cohan puts it: "The postwar 'free man' had to depend upon the state to preserve his independence in the face of the communist threat" (134), and as Elaine Tyler May notes, linking security, domesticity, and (implicitly) conformity, "in the early years of the Cold War, amid a world of uncertainties brought about by World War II and its aftermath, the home seemed to offer a secure private nest removed from the dangers of the outside world" (3).

The same economic context that produced the man in the gray flannel suit also gave rise to another form of domesticated hero: the playboy. *Playboy* magazine first appeared in December 1953 and promoted an image of masculinity that rather perversely combined domesticity and "rugged" individualism by espousing the virtues of the "bachelor pad" as the site of the endless seduction of women. It reflected the emergence of a strongly consumerist postwar society where leisure activity replaced doing or making as the basis for American masculine self-importance. (Making becomes "making out.") Within this

---

[6] This phrase comprises the title of both the novel and film, *The Man in the Gray Flannel Suit,* which appeared, respectively, in 1955 and 1956.
[7] A phrase derived from William H. Whyte Jr.'s 1956 book of the same name.

context, men were suddenly to be rewarded for doing traditional bourgeois "women's work": i.e., buying, dressing up, hanging out, and turning oneself into pleasing display.[8] Although playboy masculinity will prove much less important to my discussion of *Ulysses* than the soldier/*pater familias* opposition, it does become highly significant within one of the film's most important episodes in terms of gender.

The postwar reconfiguration of male roles along domestic, corporate, conformist, and consumerist lines provoked, as might be expected, a major crisis in American masculinity. Part of it was specifically related to the Cold War, which generated "contradictory ideals for American manhood, requiring a 'hard' masculinity as the standard when defending the nation's boundaries, yet insisting upon a 'soft' masculinity as the foundation of an orderly, responsible home life" (Cohan xii). But more broadly, the family and organization man on the one hand, and the leisure hound on the other, "call[ed] into question the traditional American myth of rugged, rebellious, and masculine American individuality" (Cohan 134), creating a powerful reaction within a culture committed to that myth. *Look* magazine published a series of essays dedicated to "The Decline of the American Male," and Robert Moskin, kicking off the series, lamented: "Scientists worry that in the years since the end of World War II, [the American male] has changed radically and dangerously; that he is no longer the masculine, strong-minded man who pioneered the continent and built America's greatness" (77).[9] Ultimately the threat to conventional "mythic" American masculinity was seen as a threat to the nation: "The cosmopolitan urban culture [which gave rise to both the gray flannel suit and the playboy] represented a decline in the

[8] For a wonderful discussion of the *Playboy* phenomenon, see Ehrenreich, chapter 4. For an excellent discussion of masculinity and consumer society, see Mort.

[9] The series appeared in 1958, hence four years after the release of *Ulysses*. Nevertheless it expresses concerns that, as several of my other sources indicate, were common throughout the 1950s. And of course they are reflected in *Ulysses*.

self-reliant entrepreneurial spirit, posing a threat to the national security that was perceived as akin to the danger of communism itself" (May 10).[10]

The redefinition of masculinity following the war led, of course, to a revaluation of women's roles: "In the wake of World War II [...] the short-lived affirmation of women's independence gave way to a pervasive endorsement of female subordination and domesticity" (May 89). Moreover, revaluation became devaluation rooted in resentment of women's briefly elevated wartime status. Philip Wylie paved the way with his 1942 *Generation of Vipers*, attacking overbearing mothers and "Momism" for turning out weak and passive sons. By 1950, *Better Homes and Gardens* was asking "Are we staking our future on a crop of sissies? ... You have a horror of seeing your son a pantywaist, but he won't get red blood and self reliance if you leave the whole job of making a he-man of him to his mother" (Fontaine 154).

Resentment and misogyny were only fueled by the growing crisis of masculinity, and by 1956 Wylie was back with a vengeance, claiming that women were actually running American corporations as well as driving men to early graves: "Their mates soon die. The insurance is made out to the gals and the real estate is in their name. They own America by mere parasitism" (29). *Look* and Moskin chipped in, threatening that "an increasing proportion of women will hold authority-wielding jobs in the future," and whining: "For a while, the male fled to the basement and busied himself sawing, painting and sandpapering. But the women followed him, and today they are hammering right along with him. No place to hide here" (77).[11]

May sees this gender backlash reflected in the cinematic representation of the times: "Two positive images of

---

[10] It must be noted that the playboy did not give rise to popular press denunciations of "sissification" in the same way as did the domesticated husband-father. However, its contribution to the general atmosphere of male crisis in the 1950s has been recognized by more recent gender critics such as Ehrenreich and Cohan.

[11] For an excellent discussion of 1950s and 1960s gender issues relevant to my discussion, see Ehrenreich.

women had shared the limelight during wartime: the independent heroine and the devoted sweetheart and wife. After the war, as subservient homemakers moved into center stage, emancipated heroines gave way to predatory female villains" (May 67). May is, of course, referring to film noir's "femme fatale," who always pays for her strength, independence, and sexuality with death or submission. This figure, as we shall see, finds its way, surprisingly enough, into *Ulysses*.

As May suggests, within the context of postwar male paranoia and misogyny, the only acceptable role for women became that of the loyal, passive, unthreatening, helpmate of men: "the 1950s version of the 'superwoman' was the wife and mother who could fulfill a wide range of occupational roles ... all within the home" (May 185).

In short, during the period in which *Ulysses* was co-produced, America was in the midst of a male re-domestication crisis that pitted two new domestic American "heroes" – the husband/father/head-of-household and the tasteful and well turned-out consumer/playboy – against the traditional undomesticated American adventurer – and that demonized women and defined acceptable femininity with extraordinarily restrictive bounds. The remainder of this essay will seek to demonstrate how the film re-presents all this, resisting the domestication of Ulysses and affirming the image of the rugged American yet, at the same time, feeling obliged to pay at least lip service to the ideology of re-domestication prevalent at the time. In each case, the goal is the re-founding of male supremacy via (ideally) the action hero outside the home and (if worse comes to worst) the patriarch within.

Ulysses,
Heroic Masculinity, and Re-domestication

One of the contradictions that emerges in *Ulysses*'s adherence to the warrior/adventurer ideal arises from the fact that Ulysses is now probably well into his forties, slowing down a bit, hence inclined towards a more domestic lifestyle. This is clear from the very fact that he is coming home at last. It surfaces when he jokes on Phaeacia about wanting a magic elixir to restore his youth, and again in his last words to Penelope in the film, promising her a "tranquil" future. However, in order to sustain the figure of the warrior/adventurer, the film must largely ignore age, and Ulysses must for the most part act 20 years younger than he really is, both on Phaeacia and on Ithaca.[12]

In this respect, *Ulysses* follows Homer's *Odyssey*, and it is one of the many ways in which the latter serves as "justification" for a re-domestication story that, in the end, heroizes the undomesticated male. In fact, the basic situation of the *Odyssey* – a returning vet "forced" to adventure for ten years, then vanquish a formidable number of enemies, all of which makes his exploits far more memorable than his reunion with family – serves as an apt point of departure for the 1950s recuperation of rugged masculinity amidst the threat of domestication. As we will see, *Ulysses* even outdoes its predecessor, diverging from it in ways that further inflate its protagonist's heroic identity.

One of the ways in which *Ulysses* undermines its re-domestication tale is by creating three role distinctions where the normal re-domestication process or crisis involves two. Instead of the soldier/adventurer vs. the head-of-household, the film offers us the wild and irresponsible vs. the more mature and sensible soldier/adventurer. The only substantive domestication that takes place is within a twofold warrior identity. Ulysses starts out as an egotistic madman who gets into needless trouble baiting the gods and is even responsible for the death of his men on Circe's island. This is all represented in flashbacks, through which Ulysses and we are able to review his delinquent past. Seemingly educated by this review, Ulysses matures into a far more disciplined figure, a pre-Rambo version of the thoroughly focused maestro of mayhem, for his return to Ithaca. We are asked to accept this transformation

---

[12] Of course Hollywood has since made this a moot point, trotting out aging John Waynes, Clint Eastwoods, Harrison Fords, James Garners, etc., as still-with-it action heroes.

Certainly the *Odyssey* is also forced, on occasion, to "rejuvenate" its protagonist; however, there is also far more indication of Odysseus as a man approaching middle age.

(though even it is not complete, as I will argue later) in lieu of the real domestication of the warrior (wild *or* tamed) into a *pater familias*.

Although, on the level of action, the postwar tension between masculine identities gets shifted from soldier/ adventurer vs. family man to good soldier vs. bad, the former resurfaces on the level of dialogue, occupying a great deal of film time. Ulysses's remarks throughout the film, particularly on Phaeacia, with Circe, and to his shipmate Eurylochus, articulate both the tension and Ulysses's clear privileging of a heroic over a domesticated identity.

Ulysses's comments on the subject arise in part in relation to his film-long quest for identity. Consistent with the proliferation of psychologies of individuation in the postwar,[13] *Ulysses* is constructed largely as a search for self. In a significant departure from the *Odyssey*, Ulysses is introduced to us as a victim of amnesia, and he spends the greater part of the film, principally through the flashbacks, trying to figure out who he is.[14] His sense of identity proves founded on two divergent things – origins and deeds, each of which entails his "name," although in significantly different ways. The issue of origins emerges as soon as Nausicaa discovers him on the beach:

> Nausicaa: Who are you? What is your name?
> Ulysses: I don't know. There's no name in my head.
> Nausicaa: You don't even know the name of your country?
> Ulysses: I remember nothing.

The issue of deeds emerges when one of Nausicaa's countrymen suggests to Ulysses that he may have been a warrior. Ulysses repeats the word, seeing if it can trigger any memories. Then he says "My name, my deeds ... Day and night I keep searching for them in the dark." Shortly later,

---

[13] The writings and teachings of figures such as C.G. Jung, Alfred Adler, and Carl Rogers were central to the theorization of individuation in this period. (See my bibliographical entries on Jung, Adler, and Rogers for introductions to their work.)

[14] In the *Odyssey* the flashbacks are Odysseus's conscious retelling of his exploits and adventures, hence there is no search for identity.

on the beach, as he stares out to sea and tries to summon up his past, he repeats in interior monologue: "My name, my deeds. Who am I? Who am I?"

Clearly these two bases for self-identification correspond (in reversed order) to the roles of family man (home, roots) and renowned soldier/adventurer. In the first instance, "name" bespeaks merely what one is called (i.e., literal identity); in the second, it connotes reputation based on actions. In the context of Ulysses's situation as a former warrior seeking his home, there is obviously the need for a transition from the latter to the former. The fact that only Nausicaa aligns his identity with origins, while he links it twice with deeds, is strong indication that no such transition is likely to occur.

Another explicit juxtaposition of the "homebody" and the warrior occurs during Ulysses's encounter with Circe. Trying to prevent Ulysses from abandoning her, Circe offers him divinity: "I shall give you something that will make you forget [your] miserable kingdom and a wife who grows old. Remain and this very night Olympus shall welcome a new god, Ulysses. This is my gift, the greatest gift that has ever been offered to a man." Ulysses responds: "No. There are greater gifts. To be born and to die and, in between, to live like a man." And he adds, "I no longer see myself falling in battle or in the fury of a storm. It will take much less. A puff of cool air, a sudden chill one night." Here Ulysses seems to be renouncing heroic exploits and choosing domestic tranquility. However, he immediately backtracks, following up on his remarks about a peaceful death with: "But even so, this vulnerable mass of fears is there to battle with the gods and has not yet been defeated. If it is that one day men shall speak of me, I hope they say with pride that I was one of them."

The most explicit instance of juxtaposition and obvious preference occurs in a shipboard conversation between Eurylochus and Ulysses. The former, always cautious and responsible, is happy to see the ship being carried steadily homeward:

Eurylochus: "There's no wind, but we have a swift current."
Ulysses: "Makes you happy, doesn't it?"
Eurylochus: "Doesn't it please you too?"

Ulysses: "I don't know. There's a part of me that loves the familiar, the end of the journey, the harbour, the cooking fires at home. There's always the other part. That part loves the voyage, the open sea, storms, strange shapes of uncharted islands, demons, giants. Yes, Eurylochus, there's part of me that's always homesick for the unknown."

Here there is no mistaking the fact that Ulysses, whatever the attractions of home might be, cannot ultimately renounce his role as adventurer or embrace an origins – rather than deeds-centered sense of self.

If Ulysses's various proclamations reveal both a tension between re- and anti-domestication and a strong tendency towards the latter, the conditions under which he must return to Ithaca push him yet further away from the former. For one thing, he returns not just as father and husband but as king of Ithaca. In addition, as I suggested before, he must revert to his role as warrior to clean out the suitors who threaten his family and his rule. Both of these derive from the poem and thus do not necessarily reflect the pressures of 1950s American ideology (except of course that this story is singled out for telling in 1950s for a largely American film production). However, there is something specific to the Camerini version of the *Odyssey* that increases the difficulty of re-domestication and dovetails with 1950s cultural issues: Ulysses must revert to fighter and killer partly because his son Telemachus is weak and ineffectual. Whereas in the *Odyssey*, with the aid of Athena, Telemachus confronts the suitors, strikes out in search of his father, undergoes an extensive process of education, and, by the end, is nearly the equal to Odysseus (able even, it would appear, to string the bow only his father can string),[15] the Telemachus of *Ulysses* goes nowhere and does nothing. His one attempt to confront the suitors is a dismal failure (in fact, Penelope's forceful address to the suitors early in *Ulysses* replaces that of Telemachus in Book 1 of Homer's epic). Their grip on the island seems at least partly the result of his helplessness.

---

[15] He does not actually do it, but he is about to when his father asks him to desist.

His utter dependence on his father's heroic strength is made clear during his reunion with Ulysses when he wants to make the suitors "quake with fear and tremble," not by confronting them himself, but by announcing "daddy's" return!

In its representation of Telemachus, *Ulysses* clearly throws its lot in with the masculinity alarmists of the 1950s, who saw only a new generation of sissies being raised as the result of the wartime absence of (he-man) fathers. Moreover the representation of Ulysses as the savior of weak and useless youth would seem to reflect a reaction of the wartime generation to fears of obsolescence now that the war is over and re-domestication has become the norm.

The film's concluding scenes provide the most compelling testimony of the warrior-family man tension and the crisis of re-domestication that I have just identified. However, I will hold off on a discussion of those scenes until the end of the essay, and until I have identified within *Ulysses* some additional consequences of that crisis.

THE DEMONIZATION AND CONTAINMENT OF WOMEN

The anxieties around masculinity evident in 1950s American society are not only reflected in the split between warrior and family man, between a strong older and a hopeless younger generation; they give rise to the same kind of female demonization noted in my discussion of 1950s American gender ideology. There is more than a hint of Momism in the relationship between Penelope and Telemachus. Not only is the latter presented as a wimp, but the one time he tries to assert himself and go off in search of Ulysses, Penelope responds "You must not leave me, stay with me my son," and buries him in a smothering embrace. Clearly, this Ithacan sissy is the product of a domineering mother. Somewhat later in the film, when Telemachus wants to take some sort of action against the suitors, another mother figure, the nurse maid Eurycleia, squelches him, saying: "we are only a woman and a young boy" and, in response to his wish to organize others, she objects: "but who? Women and boys who are too young?" (This again is a significant departure from the original.)

The major figure through whom women are negatively represented is Circe. Played by the same actress (Silvana Mangano) who plays Penelope, she is the feared dark side of the good wife and mother. She (too) is beautiful. But more importantly she is powerful, independent, and openly sexual. Moreover, she represents less a real women than Ulysses's (and 1950s male society's) fears about women. This is suggested when Ulysses muses on the similarity between Circe and Penelope ("same proud face, same dark eyes") and Circe incisively interjects, "Isn't the difference between one woman and another only in the mind of a man?" It is further implied when Circe triggers Ulysses's fears about Penelope's faithfulness, which are made all the worse by his own infidelities and by the fact that the "promiscuous" Circe is Penelope's double. He responds to Circe's comment about "difference" with "No. The difference is Penelope would never let a stranger take her in his arms." When Circe then says, "Not even a stranger like Ulysses?" he becomes extremely upset, though he quickly sublimates his anxiety by succumbing to one of Circe's kisses. Circe is "evil," then, precisely to the extent to which she serves as a mirror of Ulysses's doubts and insecurities.

Given Ulysses's swift suppression of angst in the arms of Circe, one can argue that his lengthy stay with Circe[16] derives more from his fear of going home and finding out that Penelope has someone new, than from desire for Circe per se. This interpretation is reinforced by the scene in which Eurylochus momentarily convinces Ulysses to leave. As Ulysses starts to join his men, he suddenly stops virtually in his tracks. It does not seem to be Circe's witchcraft nor even her sexual attractiveness that detains him. (When they embrace in this scene, he does not even

---

[16] In the poem, Odysseus spends seven years on Calypso's island, but the film effectively combines the Calypso and Circe episodes while radically reducing the length of Odysseus's/Ulysses's dalliance. Both the elimination of one of the women from Ulysses's wanderings and the reduction from seven years to six months would have made Ulysses's "indiscretions" more palatable given the sexual conservatism of the 1950s.

reciprocate her kiss.) It seems less that he wants to stay than that he does not want to go. Ulysses, then, is "bewitched" more by Penelope than by Circe, or more accurately by the power he bestows on Penelope through his own insecurity, infidelity, and lack of trust.

As has been suggested earlier in this essay, and as is now firmly established in feminist critique, within the logic of threatened masculinity, women's power never goes unpunished. For this reason, in the end Circe, as an independent ("bad") woman, is abandoned for the "good" Penelope.[17] Moreover, with her bleached blond hair, over-the-top dark veils and dark lashes, icy cool, self-assured, demeanor, and of course independence and sexuality, she is the reincarnation in epic guise of the always-punished (anti)heroine of film noir: the aforementioned femme fatale.[18] This confirms the ideological background of both *Ulysses* and the 1950s American re-domestication drama, for as Susan Hayward notes in reference to the femme fatale:

> in film noir, [the] construction and subsequent destruction of the sexually assertive woman must be viewed within the economic and political climate of the 1940s and 1950s ... [and] the repressed insecurity and paranoia respective to the political climate of those two decades. On the economic front, thanks to the Second World War, women went into work in the 1940s in huge numbers to help the war effort – and in many cases did so by replacing "their" men who were at war. By the end of the war, these formerly independent women were being pushed back into the family and the domestic sphere. The film noir challenged the family by its absence and so did the film noir woman who, as sexually indepen-

---

[17] Unfortunately, the film does not follow though on the signifying capacity of Mangano's Penelope/Circe to defeat the simple bad-good opposition by emphasizing the uncontainable, unpossessable difference of woman as simultaneously self and other, familiar and unfamiliar, home and foreign land.

[18] The music in Ulysses's first encounter with Circe is an ingenuous mix of the film's "epic" strains with intimations of film noir.

Circe quite literally keeps Ulysses "in the dark," shutting out the sunlight from his (and her) cave, which might well be a punning reference to the typical relationship between femme fatale and noir male protagonist.

dent, contributed to the instability of the world in which the male protagonist found himself. The . . . film noir was, then, an expression of male concern at women's growing economic and sexual independence and a fear of the men's own place in society once they returned from war. (121)

Anxieties about women are, as Momism confirms, inevitably linked to fears about feminization, and one of the ways in which Circe is demonized is through the emasculating effect she has on Ulysses. After his six months with Circe, he turns into a classic image of the effete man of leisure: bathing, primping, wearing pretty clothes, and admiring himself in the mirror. He also becomes quite childish and effeminate, making Circe more a mother than a lover. His hedonistic sex-centered lifestyle reflects the newly emergent ideology of *Playboy*, while Circe's cave is a cross between a Playboy Club (with ever attentive "bunnies")[19] and the consummate Hugh Hefner bachelor pad. The implication, of course, is that male sexuality breeds dependence on women (rather than a free-wheeling bachelor, Ulysses is a kept man), which in turn breeds infantilism, or yet another version of Momism (with woman as a sexually predatory mother). All of which signifies, obviously, the loss of manhood, accentuated by the loss of *all* the other men (i.e., Ulysses's crew) in this segment.

RE-DOMESTICATION AND THE PROPER WOMAN

As May and Hayward suggest, re-domestication has clear implications not only for masculinity but for acceptable femininity. And what better female model for domestic harmony might American postwar society have or want than Penelope.[20] She is Western culture's epitome of the passive woman, characterized over and over again by the

---

[19] Of course *Ulysses* could not have been referring specifically to Playboy Clubs. The first one did not open until 1960. However the Circe scenes capture in lifestyle and ambiance the *Playboy* phenomenon, both magazine and club.

[20] Once we move into the representation of women, gender ideology becomes less specifically American, in that the film reproduces images and expectations that are true of Western societies in general.

epithet "waiting." She is the ever faithful wife and dutiful mother (with the one limitation of promoting Momism in Ulysses's absence, which I address earlier and below), completely defined by her man even in his prolonged absence. In short, *she* is where domestication resides in the film and in American society, and her total commitment to it allows and abets Ulyssses's "natural" male wildness.

In the film, enhanced by the fact that Mangano plays both roles, Penelope represents Circe's sexuality fully contained within the family unit. Her "good" domestic asexuality is also repeatedly contrasted in the film with the "bad" sexuality of the maidservants, who are off partying with the suitors as Penelope does and undoes her tapestry. She is mother not only to Telemachus but to Ulysses himself, for she gives birth to him narratively when he appears on the beach for the first time, out of a dissolve and tilt from her image, intoning, "While I wait for Ulysses... Ulysses." What dormant or residual sexuality she might feel gets quickly sublimated then expressed only as motherhood. For, in a moment of apparent weakening she tells one of the suitors, "if you.... win, I shall not complain of having to choose a man like you" – only to retreat immediately into her role as parent: "If you really love me Antinous, I ask you one favor. One promise ... Save my son's life. He must not die ... I entrust him to you, Antinous." (Here again we have indications of Momism and Telemachus's weakness.)

Of course the containment of women's sexuality is evident from the blatant double standard that exists in the film. Ulysses is allowed to have a fling with Nausicaa, excused by his amnesia (one of the reasons, arguably, why it is introduced into the film, not having been part of the *Odyssey*). Then he gets to spend several months with Circe. But Penelope is allowed only a hint of possible yielding, and even it can be attributed to her exhaustion waiting for Ulysses rather than her own sexual desire.[21]

---

[21] Sexual containment is also evident on Phaeacia, as Nausicaa's father Alcinous responds to her emerging sexuality ("I see [a] woman taking the place of my little child") with the satisfaction of knowing that she will

The film's modeling of appropriate female behavior even includes a rather strong antidote to Momism. When Circe summons up the dead in an effort to persuade Ulysses to accept her offer of immortality, his mother unexpectedly appears, much to Circe's dismay. Anything but the overprotective type, she berates him for what we have seen to be his unmannish life with Circe: "I died waiting for you ... You have been away too long my son." (He looks down, ashamed, and says, "I know.") Then she sends him on his way to Ithaca, assuring him of Penelope's constancy ("Penelope is still waiting for you"), but even more importantly recalling him to his role as warrior: "Treachery and deceit menace your home."[22] It is on this note that Ulysses rediscovers his identity, awakens from amnesia, requests a ship from the Phaeacians, and returns to Ithaca. It is also one of the moments in which the wild and irresponsible warrior is disciplined into greater self-control and accountability.

We can deduce (at least) two things from Ulysses's encounter with his mother: women *should* be mothers (the intervention of Ulysses's mother is narratively crucial), and/but an apt mother for a "real" man is not one who coddles (Penelope without a man around the house) but one who incites to battle (or in the case of the dissolve from Penelope to Ulysses, gives birth to heroes).

ULYSSES IN ITHACA
Anybody Seen the Family Man?
The first thing to note about the Ithaca sequences is that they are, like a classic American Western, constructed to culminate with the showdown: i.e., the final "sword-out" between Ulysses and the suitors. Although there are important preceding scenes between Ulysses (disguised) and Penelope, and Ulysses and Telemachus,

---

quickly be herded into a marriage to Ulysses (a marriage that is cancelled by the return of his memory).
[22] One of the things I have not had the opportunity to address is the ideological link between *Ulysses* and American anti-Communist paranoia. The statement, "Treachery and deceit menace your home," would have resonated as a kind of anti-Communist slogan in the McCarthy era, during which the film was conceived.

these scenes are secondary, and the brief post-showdown scene, Ulysses's true reunion with Penelope, is anti-climactic and hurried, as though neither scriptwriters nor director cared much once the bloodshed ended. The relative significance of the showdown is further heightened by the fact that the film brings Ulysses home to Ithaca only at the end of his story, whereas in the *Odyssey*, he spends twelve of the twenty-four books in his homeland, doing a host of things other than wiping out his competitors. Equally important, in the original, Ulysses's revenge is followed by long and poignant scenes between him and Penelope in which he proves his identity through his knowledge of their marriage bed (clearly a major symbol of domesticity), and in which they recapture the intimacy of their past, spending a long night in bed together.[23]

Not only is reunion far outweighed by violent housecleaning, but the film (in this case emulating the epic) sutures the divide between warrior and family man by turning the home into a battlefield, a fact even Ulysses cannot overlook: "many terrible things have happened to me Telemachus, but none more terrible than to bring death into my house on the day of my homecoming." This requires that the head of the household act immediately as warrior, not husband or father. As suggested earlier, Ulysses proves an inordinately talented killer, polishing people off with bare hands, conventional weapons, or whatever ambient objects come to hand.

Moreover, in the film, Ulysses refuses to reveal himself to Penelope through anything other than acts of heroic violence. She comes to recognize him through his stringing of his bow and killing of the suitors, not through their marriage bed. This underscores her ultimate need for him more as fighter than as lover, a point she herself seems to recognize in her prayer to Athena: "The Ulysses you bring

---

[23] This is not to say that the showdown is not also dramatically crucial to the poem. And the poem includes another battle, between the family of the suitors and Odysseus, Laertes, and Telemachus, in which Odysseus again becomes defined as warrior. However, in terms of its apportioning of time, the film pushes Ulysses's identity even further in the direction of the warrior as opposed to the family man than does its source text.

back to me ... is an angry man. Forced to kill ruthlessly. Why Athena did his long road back to me have to be so bloodstained?"

While the clear emphasis in the final scenes is on Ulysses as action hero, the film cannot dismiss re-domestication altogether; its importance to 1950s America is far too great. For one thing, there is a suggestion as noted earlier that the Ulysses we see in action in Ithaca is a "kinder, gentler" warrior than the figure we have seen at Troy, on the high seas, and with Polyphemus and Circe. He plans his revenge meticulously, and he displays great patience disguised as a mendicant suffering the abuse of the suitors. Moreover, his comment about bringing death into his own home reflects a newfound awareness of the consequence of his actions. So, if we don't have the re-domestication of the soldier into the family man, we have at least the apparent domestication of the wild man-warrior. (Even this is qualified, however, because in his slaughter of the suitors, Ulysses exhibits a ferocity that hearkens back to his behavior in the flashbacks. Situating his behavior in the context of 1950s America, the message seems to be that, in the wake of two world wars and in the shadow of nuclear holocaust, men, regardless of the pressures for re-domestication, need also be capable of extreme and even irrational violence to match the irrationality of the times.)

We also have a dubious last-ditch attempt to convert the partially domesticated warrior into the homebody. First of all, Ulysses proclaims unconvincingly to Penelope: "So many years of our youth squandered in the savagery of war, in lost and confused wanderings ... I promise you, I'll make up for it in the tranquil years that lie ahead ... We'll make up for every bitter and lonely hour we both have known." Penelope then punctuates Ulysses's newfound domesticity with, "Yes, together," and the camera focuses on a tapestry depicting a man with an ox, plowing the fields. If we take the opening credit sequence and the tapestry as "lifestyle" icons, we have presumably moved from the ship and sea to home; from wandering to farming; and from life on the move to static contemplation (domestic art). All of this, however, betokens a kind of down-on-the-farm retirement that hardly computes in light of Ulysses's clearly stated homesickness for the unknown.

We can also question the authenticity of any conclusive re-domestication given what we have seen of home life earlier in the film. In the absence of sustained re-domestication scenes on Ithaca, we do have Ulysses's stay with Circe. On the one hand, its reduction of Ulysses to effeminacy and infantilism is meant to be read as the effect of his irresponsibility. On the other, it constitutes the closest thing we get to a marriage in the film, and it is equally possible to read the depressing state of Ulysses's masculinity as the result of six months' house arrest: enough to make any man (except those "pantywaists" and "sissies" reared by overbearing moms) want out of the home and back on the road.

Insecure Men and Women in Their Place

The Ithaca scenes again reveal Ulysses's insecurity and the containment of women necessary to dissolve it. Despite his mother's assurances and Penelope's own words to him disguised as a beggar ("Penelope remains faithful"), Ulysses still refuses to face her openly, telling Telemachus: "Not even she must know [I have returned]. Not until tomorrow. Then will I know if she still loves Ulysses the way she did when I left the port of Ithaca." This "test" is another of the film's departures from the original, and its patent absurdity in light of Ulysses's philandering suggests, again, that his anxiety about Penelope derives more from his behavior and concomitant guilt than from any rational concern about Penelope.

In the face of such male hysteria, women's behavior must be not only strictly monitored (Ulysses's test) but thoroughly restricted. Independent, sexual, and "bewitching" femininity, such as that represented by Circe, must be eliminated. What remains is the kind of woman who will accept Ulysses back without hesitation after twenty years of war, sex, and adventure, without any apparent effort to contact her. And even in her compliance she must be stripped of her earlier dignity and strength. She now describes herself, without irony, as Ulysses's "prize,"[24] then, in the final moments of the film, we see her, for the first time, prostrate, then on her knees. This marks a radical shift in her characterization, for throughout the film, her upright bearing, usually standing but also sitting at her tapestry, has been a compelling sign of her power and ability to resist the suitors. She has often been shot from relatively low angle and above the suitors. Even with Antinous she holds her own visually. It is with the appearance of Ulysses, even when he is still disguised, that she begins to sag and slump, and lose her visual autonomy.[25]

The narrative justification for Penelope's uncharacteristic posture is the fact she is praying to Athena, but the dramatism of the change and its association with Ulysses's return cannot help but give it an ideological significance far beyond its narrative cause. The good woman remains "upright" to all other men but melts into submission with her husband. Her collapse assures uncontested power for masculinity even if the warrior must limit his activities to the unheroic domain of the home. Hence, as I suggested above, the only real domestication that occurs in *Ulysses* lies in the utterly contained figure of Penelope, as women must pay the price for the hero's postwar return.

THE END

Having at least nodded in the direction of re-domestication in the concluding conversation between its protagonist and Penelope, *Ulysses* has to renounce it one more time and celebrate Ulysses once and for all as the

---

[24] She refers to a contest in which Ulysses strings his bow and whistles an arrow through the heads of twelve arrows lined up one after the other. He performed this feat before he went off to war and does it again as part of his vanquishing of the suitors.

[25] In the role of Circe, Mangano is never thus weakened in Ulysses's presence, a sign in part of his weakness while with her, but also a significant part of Mangano's iconographic strength until all but the final scenes.

adventuring hero.[26] The final scripted words of the film tell us:

> The dust of centuries has not dimmed the glories of Ulysses's heroic deeds. The cave of Polyphemus still reverberates with the bellowing roars of the son of Neptune. The sorrowful face of Penelope still gazes longingly across the open sea. And on a distant shore Circe still casts her spell. For the immortality that Ulysses refused of a Goddess was later given him by a poet. And the epic poem that Homer sang of the hero's wanderings and of his yearning for home will live for all time.[27]

Clearly the Ulysses who has merited the immortality of Homer's epic poem is not some homebody in a gray flannel tunic. He is the restless explorer famous for "the glories of [his] heroic deeds." He may yearn for home, but he certainly is not defined by it. Penelope is (again) reduced to stasis and mournful waiting; she has no existence apart from her man. The one thing that is ostensibly absent from the final words is masculine insecurity, though of course there is no greater evidence of it than the need to inflate men not only into heroes but virtually into gods. (Not only is Ulysses now immortal, but Homer has the power to bestow immortality.) It is this tumescent imperative that makes *Ulysses* so resistant to 1950s re-domestication, giving Ulysses his home and his heroism too, while making sure his identity derives firmly from the latter.

WORKS CITED

Adler, Alfred. *The Individual Psychology of Alfred Adler: A Systematic Presentation in Selections from his Writings.* Ed. Heinz

---

[26] In so doing, *Ulysses* is more faithful to the Western literary tradition than to Homer. In his introduction to Robert Fagle's recent translation of the *Odyssey*, Bernard Knox notes how, for figures such as Dante and Tennyson, Odysseus/Ulysses has become only "the restless explorer, the man who, discontented with the mundane life of that home he had longed for, set off again in search of new worlds," even though "these visions of Odysseus . . . have little to do with Homer's Odysseus, who wants above all to find his way home and stay there" (25).

[27] I have eliminated the spaced dots that appear the film's written text, to avoid the impression that there are elisions in the text.

L. Ansbacher and Rowena R. Ansbacher. New York: Harper-Collins, 1964.

Brunetta, G.P. *Dal neorealismo al miracolo economico, 1945-1959.* V. 3. of *Storia del cinema italiano.* 4 vols. Rome: Riuniti, 1993.

Cohan, Steven. *Masked Men: Masculinity and the Movies in the Fifties.* Bloomington: Indiana UP, 1997.

Duggan, Christopher, and Christopher Wagstaff, eds. *Italy in the Cold War: Politics, Culture and Society, 1948-58.* Oxford: Berg, 1995.

Ehrenreich, Barbara. *The Hearts of Men: American Dreams and the Flight from Commitment.* New York: Doubleday, 1983.

Ellwood, D.W., and G.P. Brunetta, eds. *Hollywood in Europe: Industria, politica, pubblico del cinema 1945-1960.* Florence: La Casa Usher, 1991.

Fontaine, Andre. "Are We Staking Our Future on a Crop of Sissies?" *Better Homes and Gardens* Dec. 1950: 154-56.

Gundle, Stephen. "L'americanizazzione del quotidiano. Televisione e consumerismo nell'Italia de-gli anni Cinquanta." *Quaderni storici* 62.2 (1986): 561-94. Qtd. and trans. in Duggan.

Hayward, Susan. *Key Concepts in Cinema Studies.* New York: Routledge, 1996.

Jung, C.G. *The Essential Jung: Selected Writings.* Ed. Anthony Storr. Princeton: Princeton UP, 1999.

Knox, Bernard. "Introduction." *The Odyssey.* Trans. Robert Fagles. Introd. and Notes by Bernard Knox. New York: Penguin, 1997. 3-67.

May, Elaine Tyler. *Homeward Bound: American Families in the Cold War Era.* New York: Basic Books, 1988.

Mort, Frank. "Boy's Own? Masculinity, Style and Popular Culture." *Male Order: Unwrapping Masculinity.* Ed. Rowena Chapman and Jonathan Rutherford. London: Lawrence & Wishart, 1988. 193-224.

Moskin, Robert J. "The American Male: Why Do *Women* Dominate Him?" *Look* 4 Feb. 1958: 77-80.

Rogers, Carl. *The Carl Rogers Reader.* Ed. Valerie L. Henderson. New York: Houghton Mifflin, 1989.

Wagstaff, Christopher. "Italy in the Post-War International Cinema Market." Duggan and Wagstaff 89-115.

Whyte, William J. Jr. *The Organization Man.* New York: Simon, 1956.

Wilson, Sloan. *The Man in the Gray Flannel Suit.* New York: Simon, 1955.

Wylie, Philip. "The Abdicating Male... and How the Gray Flannel Mind Exploits Him Through His Women." *Playboy* Nov. 1956: 29.

____. *Generation of Vipers.* New York: Holt & Rinehart, 1942.

The Portrait of a Girl:
A Reading of *Last Tango in Paris*

Cinzia DiGiulio

> It is difficult to grasp the fact that the center of male
> domination lies not in direct expressions of personal
> violence (rampant though they are) but in the societal
> rationality which may or may not be defended by men.
> Male domination, as Weber said of rationalization,
> works through the hegemony of impersonal organiza-
> tion: of formal rules that refer to the hypothetical in-
> teraction of autonomous individuals; of instrumental
> knowledge founded in the subject's control of the ob-
> ject world; of the accumulation of profit, which bows
> neither to need nor tradition. It is this protean imper-
> sonality that makes it so elusive.
>
> (Benjamin 216)

When *Last Tango in Paris* was presented for the first
time at the New York Film Festival (on October 14,
1972), it created a huge commotion. Pauline Kael, the *New
Yorker* film critic, saluted it as "a landmark in movie history. . .the most powerfully erotic movie ever made, and it
may turn out to be the most liberating movie ever made"
(Kael 27-28). At the same time, the Italian Catholic church
prosecuted *Last Tango* for obscenity, eventually having the
film banned from all Italian movie theatres and even having it sent to the stake (literally). Bertolucci's film was
eventually cleared and re-released more than ten years
later, after endless court battles.

Yet many Italians had managed in the meantime to see
the movie – that is, those who could afford to go abroad to
do so. I was among those Italians who saw *Last Tango* for
the first time in a movie theatre, in the '80s. Having had
the misfortune of seeing *Caligula* in the theatre not long
before, I was expecting something more or less on the
same wavelength: a porn flick disguised as art. I soon
found out my mistake. The sex scenes were strictly simu-
lated, played a secondary role, and were quite tame when
compared to any self-respecting skin flick, including *Caligula*. I wondered what had been so offensive for the
church. And yet, just a year or two later, a fellow graduate

student at Purdue, a devout Catholic, regretted seeing *Last Tango*, and called it "evil." Something in this movie does touch a nerve or two.

As far as my nerves were concerned, I thought that the most disturbing part must be the ending, when Jeanne shoots Paul (possibly in the groin) and kills him. God forbid women should start shooting. This was particularly true for Italy at the time the movie was made, when some extremist groups of militant feminists *were* practicing physical violence against men (one slogan recited: "Le streghe son tornate / Ma questa volta armate" – "The witches have come back / But this time they are armed"). Many an Italian boy had nightmares of being attacked and ravaged by a horde of screaming, wailing Bacchae, ready to tear him to pieces. Suburban legends for the most part, nonetheless.

Indeed, that final shot was also what Kael found so liberating. I concluded that the puzzle merited investigation. There was one problem, though: when I started my research, it seemed that most critics centered their analyses on the Brando character, Paul, while dismissing Jeanne – which was probably pretty much Bertolucci's point, after all.

Last Tango's saving grace, however, is that it *is* an art movie: it *can* and it *does* mean many things to many people. Bertolucci's movie is, thus, *obscenely* liberating because it aims at provoking a very powerful emotional response from the viewer. It is an aggressive and cruel movie, a great example of sadistic narration. To quote Kolker's excellent study, *Last Tango* in the last analysis "is not about sexuality but about the perception of sexual relationships, the structuring of emotion, and the ideology of romance, the self and the family" (125). It is especially on the aspect of the "ideology of romance" that I would like to concentrate.

Its "object" is Jeanne, the object of a threefold gaze: the hero's, the director's, and the viewer's. Through Jeanne, the viewer is constantly reminded of the politics of cinema, of the power of the camera. *Last Tango*, as we know, is a profoundly modernist movie, well rooted in self-reflexivity. It even has its resident, internal director, Tom, Jeanne's fiancé. Tom has been called "ludicrous" and "ridiculous" by most critics:[1] but this character stands for the shortcomings of classic narrative cinema and of *Last Tango* itself.[2] The TV movie he is making about Jeanne, his "Portrait of a Girl," becomes a metaphor of the movie we are watching, its double that mirrors Jeanne's oppression and her desperate struggle against it. Quite interestingly, none of the critics I have read mentioned the title of Tom's movie. By leaving that out, they can deny the centrality of Jeanne and leave her at the margin as "fool and tool" (Kolker 232): the "Portrait of a Girl" is erased to give way to Paul, and *Last Tango* is reduced to your everyday "Portrait of a Man."

Indeed, Tom's movie about Jeanne mirrors her problematic status in *Last Tango*: Tom's interest in Jeanne is a fetishist mania, a desire to film her like a Hollywood star. But there is a liberating element in his fetishizing: it is so strong, that Jeanne-fetish takes over the direction of what is done and said in the film.[3] Thus, Tom's constant pursuing of Jeanne as object of his and our gaze becomes so exaggerated as to disrupt the whole rhetoric of male, classic cinema. Another important aspect is that Jeanne always appears to be well aware of her role in Tom's movie: she is always masquerading and acting up her role of perfect female impersonator. As she says while parading in her bridal dress, "it's the dress that makes the bride," not vice versa. However, she soon shows up in the perfect outfit of a '70s feminist, leaving her beehive hairstyle in favor of a wild perm, and her miniskirt and go-go boots for a pair of pants and a jacket. It is on this occasion that she takes over the direction of her story and says: "Today we improvise."

Tom's movie also frames Jeanne's affair with Paul. After their first meeting in the "haunted-house" apartment,

---

[1] Bondanella, to quote one of the most authoritative (Bondanella 308).

[2] Bertolucci said about Tom's character that "it represents an attempt to be ironical about myself" (Ungari 89).

[3] Similarly to the *Lola Montes* example quoted by Silverman, 226. I find it extremely fascinating that Jeanne's role in Tom's movie also mirrors Maria Schneider's in Bertolucci's movie: she in fact improvised quite a large part of her character, despite the "strictness" of the script (Ungari 90).

Jeanne rushes to the station to meet Tom. They embrace and kiss each other, while being filmed by Tom's crew. As soon as Jeanne realizes that she is being "raped" by a camera, she has a violent reaction and tells Tom that he should have asked for her permission to do that. The equation "film we are watching/film Tom is making" is reinforced by the fact that, when Jeanne pushes the microphone away from her, we stop hearing what is being said until the microphone is put back to its former position (Kolker 136): what we are seeing becomes the signifier of Tom's film.

Jeanne, too, appears to be the signifier of Tom's film, but her initially negative reaction soon turns to irony and masquerade: when Tom asks her what she had been doing while he was away, she replies, very dramatically: "I thought of you day and night and I cried. Darling, I can't live without you." Jeanne is actually performing for the camera, actively provoking its intrusive gaze. Tom finds her answer "*magnifique*," seemingly unaware of Jeanne's ironic mimicking of numberless heroines of classic cinema. Indeed, Tom, being caught up in his narcissistic art, fails to really *see* Jeanne and keeps misunderstanding her (Mulvey 206).

Another instance of the undercutting of classic cinema's relation to women is Tom's shooting of his marriage proposal: he "traps" Jeanne with a life-preserver (is marriage supposed to be Jeanne's salvation or her trap?), that she throws into the water. The life-preserver immediately sinks, still leaving us the time to notice that it bears the name of Vigo's classic *L'Atalante*, a happy-ending-movie that deals with a woman's temporary marriage-crisis. Again, later on, while Jeanne tries on her bridal dress, Tom starts comparing her to a number of classic Hollywood stars: "You are better than Rita Hayworth, better than Joan Crawford, Kim Novak, Lauren Bacall, better than Ava Gardner when she loved Mickey Rooney." He does not mention any other actresses: his only touchstone for female perfection is classic cinema and its reduction of woman to object – a comparison that makes Jeanne run away (without Tom's or *our* noticing it), in her bridal dress.

At this point, I would like to highlight another curious erasure made by critics, concerning Jeanne's alleged "wedding" with Tom. For example, Kinder and Houston have claimed that Jeanne, being the "daughter of a French army colonel . . . delights in shocking her conventional mother with her liberated life style. But later she destroys her outrageous lover and chooses a conventional marriage" (Kinder and Houston 186); and Kolker: "her ultimate decision to marry Tom and adopt a safe bourgeois life signifies her ultimate betrayal of the passion Paul attempts finally, and too late, to offer her" (Kolker 135). But, in the end, Jeanne does not marry Tom: she kills Paul. Committing murder is not exactly a safe way to adopt a bourgeois life. Like her affair with Paul, Tom's film is over, too, and most likely it will never begin again (besides, Jeanne ominously tightens her lips when Tom depicts all his future films about her).

The relationship between Jeanne and Paul is, needless to say, the most disputed and interesting part of the film. They first meet on the street, during the first shot. Jeanne passes him by and stops to look at him. He has aroused her curiosity – but he is unaware of it, and does not return her gaze. Paul appears thus to be the object of Jeanne's (and the viewer's) desire, "the exotic, dangerous lover (this time a man)" (Kinder and Houston 189). She pursues him, consciously or not, to the mysterious building first, then to the phone booth, and finally to the apartment: he is always already in the place where she is going, like the Big Bad Wolf in the Little Red Riding Hood fairy-tale. Jeanne will find Paul in the apartment for rent, curled up on top of the mantelpiece, all alone in the dark, in a semi-fetal position. Jean pulls up the blinds and lets the light get in. He then moves into another room, where there is a big mysterious "thing" covered by a white sheet. He looks under it, picks up a small lamp-shade and curls up again in a corner. He hides his nose and mouth in the little cone-shaped object, and starts crying. Jeanne's curiosity reaches its peak. When the phone starts ringing, she picks it up right after Paul has answered it, and she starts overhearing the conversation.

Later on, he snaps at her for no reason, addressing her with the informal (and rude, in this case) *tu*: Paul has taken command. Instead of leaving the apartment, he comes back and – without meeting any resistance on her part – grabs her and has sex with her there and then, without a word. After that, they both leave, always without exchanging a word, taking different directions: Jeanne will go to the train station to meet Tom, who will begin shooting his "Portrait of a Girl;" Paul will return to his wife's flophouse, where we see him in a bathroom all sprayed with blood. A maid is cleaning the blood stains and telling him that the police had been there to ask her questions. We thus learn that Paul's wife is dead: she supposedly killed herself with a razor in that bathroom, the night before, without leaving any note. We also learn many things about Paul's (and Brando's) past. The maid makes a brief summary of Paul's adventurous life/Brando's adventurous career: "Then [the police] said, 'Nervous type, your boss. You know he was a boxer?' So? Then he was an actor, then a bongo player. A revolutionary in Mexico, a journalist in Japan. One day he debarks in Tahiti, wanders around, learns French..." to finally arrive in Paris and be kept by a rich wife. That's our hero's career so far: a series of central roles in classic movies, where he played the romantic rebel-hero.

Quite possibly the fact that Brando plays Paul's character helped many to see Paul in a romanticized, glamorously decadent light.[4] However, as J.C. Rice points out, these very same allusions to Brando's former interpretations aim to enhance his obsoleteness as well: yesterday's rebels have become today's oppressors, as Jeanne will soon find out. After all, it is in these years that youth culture was exhorting young people not to trust anybody over 30 – and Paul is 45.

Thus, even though Paul may be seen by some as Jeanne's "tamer" - a gratifying role for a forty-five-year-old tough guy with thinning hair and a growing tummy – his character is heavily tainted. Here are just a few superficially "motivating" traits of Paul's character, thrown in to give our hero the gloss of a fascinating, Henry-Miller-type anti-hero. First of all, he desperately needs to feel alive:

---

[4] Interestingly, Bertolucci's first choice for Paul had been Jean-Louis Trintignant, who had played the male lead in *The Conformist.*

his wife's suicide has just revealed in a most shocking way the reality and nearness of death. Moreover, when Rosa was still alive, she had a stable lover, plus several other affairs with "guests" of her hotel. Paul is now alone in the world, doesn't have any children,[5] and, last but not least, he is also culturally isolated, a stranger in a strange country, an American in Paris.[6] As Kael pointed out, "[Paul's] profane humor and self-loathing self-centeredness and street 'wisdom' are in the style of American hard-boiled fiction aimed at the masculine-fantasy market" (Kael 29). Is there any room for feminine fantasy, then?

Jeanne's affair with Paul may be seen as the fruit of her sexual fantasy, her pursuit and conquest of the dangerous, mysterious lover. Indeed another important and different aspect of Paul's character, that has often been overlooked, is that he initially appears in the guise of the Gothic villain. The first time one watches *Last Tango*, quite often one spends the first half of the movie believing that Paul has killed his wife: only in the scene when he talks to Rosa's body does one realize that he is "not guilty" of his wife's death.[7]

If Tom's use of the camera in filming Jeanne is fetishistic, the apparatus filming Jeanne with Paul – always according to Mulvey's terminology – is voyeuristic:

> Voyeurism . . . has associations with sadism: pleasure lies in ascertaining guilt (immediately associated with castration), asserting control, and subjecting the guilty person through

---

[5] We will eventually find out that he is sterile: Paul will admit in the tango ballroom that he has "a prostate like an Idaho potato," caused by "a 'nail' [he] picked up in Cuba" (Mellen 12) – possibly, also a reference to Hemingway.

[6] The parallel *Last Tango/An American in Paris* is a conscious one: "*Last Tango* is also my very own *An American in Paris*. Alongside the memory of Henry Miller begging through the streets of Montparnasse in order to eat, there is the nostalgia of a dancer who transforms his sad pilgrimage into a choreography in which he can star. When Brando enters the lift, drenched to the bone, and tip taps to let some water out of his shoes, he's my version of Gene Kelly" (Ungari 91).

[7] – and only partly at that: not by chance, in the dead chamber, Paul addresses Rosa as a "fake Ophelia drowned in the bathtub," thus automatically becoming the fake Hamlet that drove her to her death.

punishment or forgiveness. The sadistic side fits well with narrative. Sadism demands a story, depends on making something happen, forcing a change in another person, a battle of will and strength, victory/defeat, all occurring in a linear time with a beginning and an end. (Mulvey 205).

Paul "the tamer" appears to be violent from the very start. His initial angry exclamation, his blunt and aggressive attitude towards Jeanne on their first meeting, his ill treatment of the hotel maid – these are all clues that reveal the anger inside him, a violence vented against those who cannot fight back.

This *film noir* – and Gothic novel – undercurrent (i.e., Paul as the villain-murderer) remains a constant throughout the movie. The very apartment where Jeanne and Paul meet has elements of a haunted house. It is in an old building in Rue Jules Verne,[8] a fantasy place. Jeanne's entrance in the building is very ominous and reminds us of many a Gothic tale. When Jeanne first rings the front-door bell, nobody answers. The concierge is a strange woman who talks in riddles and warns Jeanne that "strange things happen in [that] place." The people who live there appear to be quite strange, too – more dead than alive: as the concierge talks, a door opens and a bare, trembling female arm deposits an empty bottle of liquor outside (this will surface again in Paul's tale about his alcoholic mother). Besides, continues the concierge-prophetess, the building is rat-ridden. As she gives her the key (a double, since the original had mysteriously disappeared), she grabs her hand and does not want to let go. Then, when Jeanne manages to free herself from the strange guardian of the place, she runs toward the old elevator, which is automatically and silently coming to fetch her, without having been called. Finally, as she enters the dark, threatening apartment, she finds her Lovelace.

Or was it Rochester, instead? Jeanne intentionally returns to the apartment, with the excuse of returning the key, and finds Paul there. The game has begun. We ini-

---

[8] The allusion to Verne is conscious, as Bertolucci has modified the geography of Paris to fit his needs (Kline 109).

tially see her going on all fours like a big cat. Some workers have just delivered a bed and few other things. But, in
case Jeanne had ever thought she might be with Paul like
Jane with her Rochester, she was mightily mistaken. If
Tom doesn't see, Paul doesn't listen. Paul is the one and
only master of the house. He immediately orders her to
take off her coat and help him out with the furniture: she
obeys meekly. Jeanne asks him to tell her his name, but
he refuses, setting the rules of the game:

> I don't wanna know nothing, nothing, nothing about you . . .
> You don't have a name, I don't have a name . . . We don't
> need names here . . . You and I are gonna meet here, without
> knowing anything that goes on outside here.

He then asks Jeanne if she is scared by his proposal. She
says no and invites him to go with her.

Many, following the "explanations'" given by Bertolucci
on different occasions,[9] have seen Paul's "rules" as a positive, utopian attempt to go back to a blissful and lost state
of 'oneness'. Kolker, for example, sees Paul attempting "to
create a world of sexuality isolated from the outside world,
to deny social identity and lineage by refusing names, to
retreat from the symbolic realm of the I and the Other"
(Kolker 189). From this point of view, Paul's later behavior
would be more of a schizophrenic slip into the symbolic.
From Jeanne's point of view, though, Paul's utopian project was reserved only for himself: he never stops seeing
her as his "fool and tool." Paul's and Jeanne's relationship
seems to follow, then, the sadomasochistic pre-Oedipal
model described by Benjamin, in which the sadist/Paul
strives to find a "surviving other."[10]

Indeed Rosa has not survived – and the bathroom covered with blood can become the scene of Paul's rebirth

---

[9] See, for example, Bachmann's in his interview of Bertolucci (page 4 and
following).

[10] "The adult sadist. . .is searching for a surviving other, but his search is
already prejudiced by his childhood disappointment with an other [the
mother] who did not survive. Likewise, the adult masochist continues to
find an other who survives, just as she did in childhood, but again loses
herself in the bargain" (Benjamin 68).

into a new struggle to overpower the Mother. His retreat into the womb-like apartment (whose strange yellow light takes possession of everything, as if it were immersed in amniotic fluid) is a desperate search for himself, albeit at the expense of an other that he is unable to recognize. Paul does not want to know anything about Jeanne, as she is just the object of his will; his unrevealed name keeps his identity separate. Paul's aggressiveness and isolation will emerge again in the next scene, when he faces Rosa's mother.[11]

Immersing themselves again in the maternal womb, Paul and Jeanne try out their pre-Oedipal language, exchanging animal-like grunts and squeaks. Still, the counter-shot links their cries with those of the animals that Tom's crew are filming – a reminder that Paul's and Jeanne's are nonetheless just conscious imitations. In this next scene, we see Jeanne telling her story in Tom's movie: her childhood in her parents' country house. We meet her nurse Olympia, "the personification of domestic virtue: faithful, economic, and racist," as Jeanne describes her. We also see pictures of "The Colonel," Jeanne's dead father, in his full army uniform. Interestingly, though, Jeanne does not talk about him in Tom's film: she will do so in the apartment, in Paul's presence: "The Colonel had green eyes and shiny boots. I loved him like a god. He was so handsome in his uniform!" To which Paul retorts: "What a steamy pile of horseshit. All uniforms are horse-shit." After this severe reprimand, Jeanne asks him again what she is supposed to say and what she is supposed to do: Paul answers with his silence.

In this long and central scene, both our heroes end up telling each other/us some revealing aspects of their past: Paul recalls his childhood with a violent father, a "super-masculine, bar-fighting, whore-fucking drunk," and a po-etic, alcoholic mother who "taught him to love nature," and who ended up in jail for walking on the street naked. Paul then asks Jeanne to tell him about her first orgasm,

---

[11] In this scene, a wide space separates them, with a door in the middle bearing the sign "Private."

although he soon shows an affected disinterest. Why? It may be that he wishes to tease and demean her ("I don't listen because whatever you say does not matter to me anyway"). This is Jeanne's interpretation. She retorts: "Why don't you listen? . . . Your solitude weighs on me . . . you are not generous, you're an egoist!" But Paul also does not want to listen because Jeanne reached her first orgasm by herself, while running to school: she achieved it in isolation, without the need for a penis – enjoying her body in public, like the naked body of Paul's mother. Paul's dismay turns into open tears when Jeanne, in a moment of self-assertion ("I can be by myself, too"), starts masturbating. Paul does not look at her and repeats his movements of the first apartment scene: he returns to his little womb-like lamp-shade, hides his face in it, and starts crying. But he immediately regains his assertive power in the next scene: while he is lying on a couch back in the flophouse, Rosa's mother comes to cuddle him and comfort him: "You're not alone, Paul." Paul first bites her hand, then scares her and the entire hotel by switching off the electric power.

The sadist, as we have already mentioned, always aims at a "togetherness" in which he can affirm his separation from the other/object. Back to the apartment, in the bathroom (Jeanne is putting on make-up, Paul is shaving) Paul remarks how he likes the old-fashioned sink of their apartment: it has a large mirror, in which Paul can gaze at himself and Jeanne at the same time, thus being reassured of his separate identity and of her being a mere impersonal image. The use of the camera reinforces this process by substituting itself for the mirror: Jeanne, completely naked, turns towards the camera, while Paul is still shaving, facing the mirror: Jeanne's [objectified] body is still a reflection, but this time of our gaze. On this occasion, Jeanne tries again to find out something about Paul's identity, but her attempt is once again frustrated. When she tries to say something about her identity, Paul yells at her. "You hate women," Jeanne says. "What have they done to you?" Paul's answer seems to come out of a handbook: "Either they pretend to know who I am, or they pretend I don't know who they are, and that's very boring." Paul can only know *who* they are *not*.

After the scene in the Paris underground (in which Jeanne gives vent to her self-reflexive frustration), the camera takes us to the flophouse, where Paul goes to visit Rosa's lover Marcel. They talk about Rosa, a scene that prepares us for Paul's dramatic monologue in the death-chamber. He leaves Marcel, muttering a spiteful "I wonder what she ever saw in you." The next shot is still a door opening: but, instead of seeing Paul walking out of Marcel's room, we see Jeanne walking into the apartment. Thinking that nobody is home (but, as usual, Paul is there - he simply had not answered her call), she walks next to the huge white "thing" and says: "Hi, monster...Something wrong?" It is quite an ironic greeting, when seen in retrospect: because this will be the notorious "butter scene." This most powerful and shocking scene, that seems to come straight out of a Marquis De Sade tale, reveals the movie's double standard in all its obscenity. Paul orders Jeanne to fetch him the butter from the kitchen and uses it soon after to sodomize her against her will.[12] But this is not all: while he is sodomizing her, he forces her to repeat after him the following catechism lesson about the "holy family": "A holy institution, meant to breed virtue in savages . . . Holy family . . . Church of good citizens . . . Where the will is broken with repression . . . Where freedom is assassinated by egotism . . . The family . . . You, fucking family . . ." We can here recognize two aspects of Benjamin's pre-Oedipal sadist: the enjoyment of anal sex as denial of the feminine organs,[13] and the use of rationality as a substitute for affect.[14] We can also interpret this scene as Paul's repetition of the primal scene, when his own "will" was broken with repression by the "fucking family." But the most intriguing aspect of this scene is what Paul is saying to Jeanne while raping her: quite paradoxically, he is "teaching" her freedom while

---

[12] It is quite interesting to note that the sodomy part was not in the original script (Bachmann 7).
[13] "The anal allusions degrade what woman has to offer, her bodily difference from man" (Benjamin 77).
[14] "This rationality bypasses real recognition of the other's subjectivity" (Benjamin 76).

denying it to her, while showing her that she is not free. *Voilà* the most subtly perverted torture for Jeanne and the empathic viewer: it is the scandal of paternalism.[15]

Jeanne is immobilized once again in the next scene, this time by Tom's *Atalante* life-saver. Then, finally, we see Jeanne's mother for the first time (although we had already met her double, Jeanne's nurse): both Jeanne's mother and Olympia are preparing, as it were, turning their country-house into a family museum in honor of the dead Colonel. M.me the Colonel is sending to the country all his things, save for the two main symbols of power: the Colonel's boots and his gun. The feeling of permanence of patriarchal power is heightened by her apparently innocent remark, while brushing the Colonel's uniform: "These military things never get old." Jeanne masquerades by trying on her father's uniform: in the next scene, she will become the bride in Tom's movie.

After running away from Tom in the pouring rain, Jeanne returns again to Paul, to suffer new degradation. Paul makes fun of her bridal dress, picks her up and lays her on the bed, next to a dead rat (this image will return in Rosa's death-chamber: she too is wearing a bridal dress). In spite of all this, Jeanne breaks into a passionate declaration of love. She is next seen completely nude, in the bathtub; Paul is washing her and "schooling" her at the same time about the impossibility of finding true love. A most interesting "slip"[16] takes place in Paul's speech:

> You want this golden, shining, powerful *wife* to build a fortress so you can hide in. So you don't ever have to be afraid . . . or you don't have to feel lonely . . . you never have to feel empty . . . Well, you'll never find him . . . you're all alone and you won't be able to be free of that feeling until you look death right in the face. . .

---

[15] I find this scene to be the most politically charged in the movie: a very effective as well as brutal reminder of how masters teach freedom to their slaves.

[16] Kline eliminates this "mistake" by substituting "wife" with "warrior" (Kline 116); Kolker corrects it with "knight" but puts the original in footnote: "Paul actually says 'wife' here, but that makes no sense in the context of the statement" (Kolker 231).

Paul is, once again, talking about himself, repeating his anguished quest for the Other that will not make him feel lonely. He finally manages to look death right in the face: first by gazing at Rosa's face, then by dying himself. But, before that, he performs one last act of sadism on Jeanne: he makes her switch roles with him, ordering her to sodomize him with her fingers, while depicting nightmarish love-tests that he would ask her to perform to prove her complete submission. Jeanne agrees to everything, "and more than that." Has she been tamed and subjugated, is she no longer threatening? In theory, "once the tension between subjugation and resistance dissolves, death or abandonment is the inevitable end of the story" (Benjamin 65). Indeed, when Jeanne returns to the apartment, Paul is not there. All rooms are empty, save for the one with the "thing," the big white monster. In a final, desperate attempt to recover from this new denial of her self, Jeanne pulls down the white sheet covering the "thing" and kicks down what is under it: a pile of discarded objects – the rubbish of the past, just like Paul turned out to be. Paul, Jeanne's symbol of rebellion against bourgeois society, turned out to be a reduplication of patriarchal oppression. Thus, what lies beneath is just one big pile of junk, under which Jeanne hides herself to cry.

Once she walks out of the apartment/womb, she is reborn a different Jeanne. As soon as Paul approaches her on the street, she starts repeating "It's over:"[17] Paul can only exist in her fantasy, or not at all. As we mentioned earlier, Paul's great attraction was in his "utopian" project, "his effort to escape society and start a new one based on 'nature', on the Romantic notion of noble savagery" (Bundtzen 181). However, his utopian dream was built on Jeanne's body and on her submission. . . So . . . Why does she shoot him? Out of anger? Out of fear? Both? We cannot say – Bertolucci doesn't let us. The one clue he left in

---

[17] Which makes me disagree with those critics who see her rejection of Paul as "class-conscious."

an interview, was that Jeanne is not supposed to represent the woman of the future, but that she is, rather, the woman of today, i.e., of the early '70s (Mellen 12). Jeanne was, in a sense, a borderline woman. As we know, Bertolucci was in those years steeped in Marxist and Freudian theories: both of them were under attack and soon to be thoroughly analyzed and critiqued by feminist thought. However, he felt the need of claiming that he was all in favor of women's liberation (Mellen 12).

One characteristic that critics have seen in Bertolucci's work was his nostalgia for situations that stop short of change, situations that come "before the revolution."[18] Jeanne's situation is quite similar. She is the woman "before the revolution," not yet fully conscious of her status: after all, she's not even in her twenties, yet. This may be the movie's greatest shortcoming: although Bertolucci wanted to create a situation of clash between two opposite forces (Bachmann 4), he pitted a middle-aged pseudo rebel against a middle-class teenager who ends up being called a bimbo. Jeanne wasn't given much of a chance as a character in the first place: how could she teach that old dog new tricks? Thus, all we are left with at the end of the movie is a curled-up, dead body, a smoking gun, and a young little witch soon to be arrested by the police. It sounds like the parable of a film director's fears of a women's revolution.

WORKS CITED

Bachmann, Gideon. "Every Sexual Relationship is Condemned. An Interview with Bernardo Bertolucci apropos *Last Tango in Paris*." *Film Quarterly* . 26 (1973): 2-9.
Benjamin, Jessica. *The Bonds of Love. Psychoanalysis, Feminism, and the Problem of Domination.* New York: Pantheon Books, 1988.
Bondanella, Peter. *Italian Cinema from Neorealism to the Present..* New York: Continuum, 1988.
De Lauretis, Teresa. *Alice Doesn't. Feminism, Semiotic, Cinema.* Bloomington: Indiana University Press, 1984.

---

[18] For a fuller discussion of this point, which has very interesting psychoanalytical implications, see Bundtzen.

Fisher, Jack. "*Last Tango in Paris*: The Skull Beneath the Skin Flick." Atkins, T.R., ed. *Sexuality in the Movies*. Bloomington: Indiana University Press, 1975. 221-32.

Kael, Pauline. *Reeling*. Boston: Little and Brown, 1976.

Kinder, Marsha and Beverle Houston. "Bertolucci and the Dance of Danger." *Sight and Sound*. 42 (1973): 186-91.

Kline, T. Jefferson. *Bertolucci's Dream Loom. A Psychoanalytic Study of Cinema*. Amherst: The University of Massachusetts Press, 1987.

Kolker, Robert Phillip. *Bernardo Bertolucci*. New York: Oxford University Press, 1985.

Mellen, Joan. "Sexual Politics and *Last Tango in Paris*." *Film Quarterly* 26 (1973): 9-19.

Mulvey, Laura. "Visual Pleasure and Narrative Cinema." *Narrative, Apparatus, Ideology. A Film Theory Reader*. ed. Philip Rosen. New York: Columbia University Press, 1986.

Rice, Julian C. "Bertolucci's *Last Tango in Paris*." *Journal of Popular Film*. 3 (1974): 157-72.

Silverman, Kaja. *The Subject of Semiotics*. New York: Oxford University Press, 1983.

Ungari, Enzo. *Bertolucci by Bertolucci*. Trans. by Donald Ranvaud. London: Plexus, 1987.

Transforming Interest:
How to Teach Students to Write about Italian American Culture

Kenneth Gulotta
TULANE UNIVERSITY

In using an Italian American theme to teach Freshman Writing, I have predictably discovered in my students a willingness to accept stereotypes of Italian Americans. Since I have expected their willingness to accept stereotypes, I have also attempted to prepare for it by researching literature on pedagogical responses to such attitudes. However, in researching the use of multicultural materials in the classroom, I have somewhat surprisingly discovered that this phenomenon seems, to some extent, to be reflected in the larger academic and critical community. The following paper discusses this dynamic and the specific problems it creates in the Freshman Writing classroom, then moves on to discuss my solutions to these problems.

In general, Freshman Composition brings to mind the specters of rhetoric, those elements of writing, such as thesis and argument, for which we must somehow inspire interest and engagement. This focus creates the impression that freshman writing classes are homogenous, that they generally follow the same structure in which the same issues and problems surface. Those of us who teach the classes, however, know that they are not all alike. In fact, they differ at the most basic levels of course structure. In *The New St. Martin's Guide to Teaching Writing*, Robert Connors and Cheryl Glenn advise in their first sentence that "The first thing any new teacher must do is gather information" (3), going on to state that a major piece of this information is "whether there is a standardized departmental structure for the course" (4). This factor determines not only the methods that are used to teach a freshman writing course, such as assignments, lectures, and peer reviews, but also the content that is used as a structure for presenting those methods. Different content, different themes make for different classes: even if we write the same types of assignments and present the same

ideas about composition, different issues arise. The choice
of a theme thus becomes a pedagogical question, since it
provides the forum to help students develop the critical
perception that makes them better thinkers and writers.
To make this forum work, we must do two things: foster
whatever initial basic interest the students have for the
subject matter and provoke a subsequent critical interest
that will help them write about the subject from different
perspectives.

For the first of these tasks, the theme of the Italian
American cultural experience is an unqualified success.
Since using an Italian American theme, I have found that
the students who sign up for my class are interested in
discussing the topic on the very first day. Previously, when
I used other themes – such as "Genre and Language" – I
had to generate interest for the topic in my students. Now,
students come to my class with opinions and questions
that make our critical examination of issues and texts
more dynamic.

Of course, there are problems with the nature of the
interest that my students show on the first day of class,
problems that can make the second task, that of inspiring
them to approach issues from a variety of critical perspectives, more difficult. A class that involves the Italian
American cultural experience can not avoid the stereotype
of the Mafioso, since, as Stephen S. Hall states in his article "Italian Americans: Media Perceptions," "the connection is so firmly established in the popular imagination,
and in the minds of people who bring information into our
homes, that it is virtually impossible to discuss the Italian
American ethos...without referring to the problem of the
Mafia" (64). However, if we are to develop the critical skill
in our students that will allow them to write intelligently
about the Italian American cultural experience, we must
concentrate on the constructs of Mafioso and Godfather as
stereotypes. We must help our students develop the ability
to examine such stereotypes and analyze how different
authors, filmmakers, and thinkers have explored and re-
acted to them. Any other attitude in the writer allows him
or her only to scratch the surface of these constructs.

Granted, other types of classes may focus on other
valuable issues. For instance, in freshman writing classes

that focus on the study of film, students may write about
Francis Ford Coppola's *The Godfather* and concentrate on
issues of cinematography – the use of lighting, music,
camera perspectives, and so on. However, in doing so,
they learn about the use of such film techniques, instead
of learning about Italian American culture. To learn about
the culture, students must directly examine how stereotypes move around and within it.

The primary trap to avoid is the widespread urge in
students to celebrate the stereotype and minimize attitudes of criticism. To counter this urge, I must present the
issue directly, but indicate that our focus will be an examination of the stereotype that will lead to a broader discussion of the Italian American cultural experience.
Therefore, I include this information in my course description, telling my students directly that we will examine
the Godfather myth and attempts by Italian Americans to
overcome it:

> *Talking with the Godfather: Italian-American Culture and the
> Mafia Stereotype.* You probably know the following story:
> Michael Corleone, born into a Mafia family, tries to escape
> his destiny, but is forced by circumstances and his own
> character to accept his mantle as Don. Any thought of
> Italian-American culture inevitably calls to mind the scenario
> portrayed in Mario Puzo's novel and Francis Ford Coppola's
> film *The Godfather*. Indeed, many works by Italian-American
> authors and artists either react to Puzo's novel and
> Coppola's adaptation of it or point out the cultural stereo-
> types that make these works so compelling to so many peo-
> ple. In this course, we will examine the Godfather myth and
> attempts by Italian Americans to explore it or overcome it.

Having been straightforward in my description of my
class, I generally expect that my students will know at the
beginning of the semester that a critical attitude about the
Godfather stereotype will be expected. Some of them, usually about thirty percent of each class, do have this knowledge. The others, however, generally have certain preconceptions that block critical thinking. My job is to help
them overcome these preconceptions.

Such students have signed up for the course because
they are interested in some of the books and films it will

use, but their interest tends to fall into the patterns of the stereotype itself: they consider a book or film "more" Italian American when it spends more of its time describing the life of the gangster. In order to make these students better writers, I must manipulate their existing interest in the stereotype of the Mafioso. That is, I must use the tension created by their celebrative interest, transforming it into an interest that will allow them to write critically about the Mafioso stereotype, as well as discover other structures within the texts and films that are worthy of critical study. The resolution of this tension is the deciding factor in teaching my students to write argumentative papers. It is a tension that is specific to the use of an Italian American theme and it is a tension that creates both obstacles and opportunities for the learning process.

When I say that this tension is specific to the use of an Italian American theme, I do not wish to ignore the efforts made by advocates of multiculturalism to reform the writing curriculum. In fact, many authors have cited the value of using multicultural themes in writing classes. On one side of the issue is the contention that the use of multicultural materials is necessary for the evolving student population. For example, in "Waking Up to the World: A Multicultural Approach to Writing," Ralph D. Story considers the use of multicultural materials a means of inspiring students of various ethnic backgrounds to similar accomplishments: "It is...essential that young African American, Latino, and Native American students be exposed to writers who come from the same culture as they do, maybe even 'look like them,' so they can discover that one doesn't have to be a Caucasian to be a writer" (193). However, Story also presents the other side of the issue, noting that the use of multicultural materials is valuable regardless of the ethnic composition of the classroom, since multicultural readings tend to offer useful ways to introduce fertile topics for writing: they "serve as catalysts for writing that transcends 'an assignment...' [by] discussing issues (e.g., race, racism, ethnocentrism, bigotry) that most contemporary writers purposely avoid" (192). Thus, even courses that do not use specific themes tend to address multicultural issues. In fact, some authors consider these issues to be the very heart of writing and learning to write. Elizabeth Robertson and Bruce K. Martin, for instance, feel that literature and writing have inherent qualities that connect them to issues of multicultural reform:

> There are persuasive arguments for concluding that the fields of writing and literature have natural affinities with each other, since both speak at some level to the difficulty of "voicing" and the possibility – even necessity – of multiple identities, as well as engagement with the "other," whether the "other" is something within or without a culturally constructed "self." In rethinking the ways in which we told and retold our experiences, we are looking at those moments of cultural tension that – by confronting us and our students with our sometimes intractable differences – provide the richest possibilities for understanding what "change" might entail. (454)

These authors demonstrate the substantial agreement within the community of writing teachers that writing about a culture, whether it is one's own or another's, naturally brings up issues and questions that, with the proper critical attention, can inspire students to attempt greater levels of understanding and expression. They suggest that the issues surrounding cultural differences naturally produce classroom tactics geared toward generating critical interest and sophisticated argument.

However, practical ideas about how we are to create productive critical attention are actually somewhat lacking from the discussion. This is unfortunate, given that the creation of such attention, which allows students to discuss ethnic stereotypes as social constructs, is always a crucial factor in teaching writing, particularly when multicultural topics are involved. Another element that appears to be lacking from current scholarship on multiculturalism and the writing curriculum is the mention of the Italian American experience as a viable culture for examination. Consider, for example, the specificity with which Story mentions useful multicultural materials:

> As an undergraduate I had the opportunity to read Gabriel García Marquez, the great Colombian writer, many years before he achieved world acclaim; I was also able to

make numerous literary explorations of the works of Leopold
Senghor (Senegalese), Octavio Paz (Mexican), Ezekial
Mphalale (black South African), García Lorca (Spanish),
Isaac Singer (Jewish), Nicolas Guillén (Cuban), Vine Deloria
(Native American), Alurista (Latino American), Aime Cesaire
(Martiniquian), Amiri Baraka (African American), and
countless other writers. (190)

The level of detail in the above list is admirable, but the
omission of Italian American writers – or the submerging
of them within the category of "countless other writers" –
highlights a lack of consideration for them as candidates
for cultural analysis. The implication is that Italian American culture is straightforward, that we will not gain the
same benefits by examining the issues contained within it
that we would from an examination of other cultures.

This lack of consideration seems to be connected to
the tendency that I see among my students to accept, with
little questioning, the stereotype of the Mafioso. In *Blood of
My Blood: The Dilemma of the Italian-Americans*, Richard
Gambino identifies such assumptions as part of a newer,
more insidious form of discrimination: "the more recent
discrimination against Italian-Americans has become re-
spectable. It is no longer the bigotry of redneck types...
The more damaging bigotry today is that shown by educated middle- and upper-class Americans" (305). When we
encounter this form of discrimination, given that it occurs
in people we would generally consider receptive to other
ideas, we might ask ourselves, why not simply confront
these students with historical information that disproves
the stereotype and let them go from there? The answer is
that we *should* present such information – such as statis-
tics about actual Italian American involvement in general
criminal activity and the involvement of other ethnic
groups in organized crime – but that this presentation
alone does not improve our initial situation. With such
information, students tend to construct one of two sim-
plistic theses: either "*The Godfather* is wrong" or "Even if
the stereotype is wrong, *The Godfather* deals with one
family only and it is entertaining."

In fact, even when they do present one of these theses,
many students merely accept such information and continue to celebrate the stereotype. They think of entertain-

ment as an arena separate from the rest of the cultural field. In this arena, stereotypes are acceptable because they provoke viewer or reader interest. Students tend to downplay the effect or power of these stereotypes in "the real world" after the last page of the novel is turned or the screen goes dark. Most beginning college students, even when they are aware of ethnic stereotypes, initially lack the ability to see such stereotypes as constructs that move through various areas and levels of culture and society, retaining associations from each context and growing in response.

Unfortunately, the presence of Italian American students in my classroom does not always circumvent this trend. It is so prevalent that its attitudes are often held by Italian Americans themselves, so that they respond at least as strongly, if not more so, than members of other ethnic groups to the stereotypes presented in *The Godfather*. Like others, they find it difficult, regardless of the quality of the prose, to resist the dramatic lure of the book, in which "Puzo wrapped the prized Italian emphasis on family cohesiveness in a marketable, criminal package to create...both the bane of Italian Americans and a cultural icon" (Hendin 144). In their attraction to the force of the characters in the novel, to the exotic appeal of a mythic Italian heritage that seems foreign even to them, my Italian American students are all too willing to accept the idea of criminal activity as a necessary thread within the heritage. This attraction initially seems to blind my students, Italian American or otherwise, to elements in stereotypes of Italian Americans – such as a propensity to criminal activity or a loss of sexual control – that they are quick to identify in stereotypes of other ethnic groups.

Thus, while students who enter a classroom to discuss multicultural works by the authors cited in Story's list tend to assume that they will be expected to look beyond the surface level of any of the associated stereotypes, my students enter with a need to witness the existence of the stereotype and a need to learn that it can be questioned. By using their existing interest, I am able to hold their attention. By then luring them into questioning their existing interest, I hope to teach them to be better, more thorough readers and, as a consequence, better, more thor-

ough writers. In the process, I hope to dispel some of the
ease with which existing stereotypes about Italian Americans maintain their hold, leading my students into other
Italian American subjects and endeavors.

To accomplish these tasks I must structure my course
carefully, giving attention to practical tasks that will generate critical attention in my students. As I require my
students to write at more sophisticated levels and at
greater lengths, I also demand that they address more
complex issues about the Godfather stereotype and Italian
American culture. My first tactic is the presentation of my
syllabus (see Appendix Item 1). I include within it the basic ideas that I present in my course description, but I
also elaborate on them, showing students how they will be
expected with each paper and assignment to know more
about the cultural issues that we are examining as well as
be able to weigh more of these issues against each other. I
try to use my syllabus for the purpose suggested by Shari
Stenberg and Amy Lee in their article "Developing Pedagogies: Learning the Teaching of English," to construct a
model of the teaching relationship that I will set up with
my students:

> In the syllabus, the teacher works to constitute her "teaching
> self" in relation to a group of students she has of yet only
> imagined. It can be read, then, for the (implicit) assumptions
> it makes about who the students are and what they are
> thought to need. Syllabi often further indicate not only what
> students will need to *acquire* or *do* to successfully engage in
> the course, but also what kind of students they are expected
> to *be*. (332)

During my discussion of the syllabus, I indicate to my
students that through the action of writing papers,
through increasing their knowledge of the class topic by
writing about it at increasing levels of complexity, they will
enhance their ability to participate in class discussions
and exercises. Thus, I indicate that learning about the
content of the class and learning to write are inextricably
linked, that students can not hope to accomplish one of
the tasks without accomplishing the other.

In order to assure students that we will discuss the
Italian American cultural experience from more than one

angle, I go over the books that we will read and analyze
and that they will write about. During this discussion, I
explain the role of the second novel that they read, Tina
De Rosa's *Paper Fish*. My discussion of this novel and my
reasons for including it in the course – that it is from the
point of view of a female narrator and deals with an Italian
American family uninvolved in any kind of criminal activity – sets off some of the issues of stereotype that they will
be expected to address in our discussion of both Puzo's
and Coppola's *The Godfather*. The attention that I give to
my syllabus enables me to accomplish two major tasks: to
set up a consistent connection between the act of writing
and the act of critical questioning in the minds of my students and to make sure that each assignment uses skills
that were developed in previous ones.

In order to maintain this connection between the act of
writing and the act of questioning, it is necessary to have
students start writing and questioning stereotypes of Italian Americans as early as possible in the semester. To
help fulfill this need, I have developed a writing diagnostic
that highlights the topic of the class (see Appendix Item 2).
I also use the diagnostic as a tool for developing revision
skills. On the first day of class, I present my syllabus and
discuss paper-writing basics. On the second day of class,
however, I begin preparations for the diagnostic and revision period. I give a lecture on reading critically, focusing
on reading as an active process, rather than the passive
event that young students typically conceive it to be. Then,
as an in-class exercise, I have my students use the reading tactics that we have discussed, such as previewing
(scanning a document for key transitions and cues for understanding), responding (making annotations on a document of personal reactions and ideas), and reviewing
(summing up ideas about a document in a paragraph or
two), to read Raymond Hernandez's article, "Congresswoman Takes a Whack at *The Sopranos* Stereotype." We
discuss the fact that these reading tactics, with their focuses on preliminary reader attitudes, line-by-line reader
reactions, and final reader synthesis, help not only to
break down and understand the article's claims and evidence, but also to identify personal attitudes that could
impair understanding.

Then, we watch Episode Ten of *The Sopranos*, "A Hit Is
a Hit" – an episode that is particularly suited to questioning the idea of the mafioso, since it blurs the lines of the
stereotype by placing Italian American gangsters in conflict with a successful gangster rapper. I instruct my students to take notes on the episode while they are fresh
from the act of critically reading the article, so that they
can learn to focus the same sort of attention on a different
medium, one that, because it is visual, requires that they
make an even greater effort to respond actively in order to
maintain critical awareness.

At the end of class, I assign a writing diagnostic that
requires my students to join the recent debate about
HBO's *The Sopranos* and how the entertainment industry
portrays Italian Americans. They must respond to Representative's Marge Roukema's criticisms of *The Sopranos*,
supporting their opinions with specific evidence from Episode 10. They may agree or disagree with her, or agree
with some points and disagree with others. The main goal
is that they make a claim about how ethnic stereotypes
function, using specific bits of textual evidence to support
their views.

On the third day of class we have a discussion about
the dynamic of ethnic stereotypes, using the episode as a
means of discussing how members of an ethnic group
have stereotypes inflicted on them by members of other
ethnic groups, but also how members of an ethnic group
may begin to use the stereotypes that are inflicted on
them as tools against the inflictors. At this end of this
class I have the students write the following first journal
assignment of the semester: "Write for fifteen minutes
about Episode Ten of *The Sopranos*, using it as evidence to
support Roukema's views. Then write for another fifteen
minutes, using the episode to counter her views." Thus,
early in the semester I require that my students make an
effort to see an issue from more than one point of view,
concentrating on the need to present clear evidence for
whatever view they support, rather than resorting to mere
personal opinion or reaction. I also give them the chance
to brainstorm ideas for the diagnostic assignment and re-
ceive feedback.

My students turn in their writing diagnostics on the

fourth day of class, when we discuss issues of thesis, argument, and analysis. I read the diagnostics before the
fifth class, so that I can discuss areas of strength and areas of concern with the class as a whole. I also use the
diagnostics to illustrate to my students why certain ideas,
such as a television show being exempt of criticism because it is intended for entertainment only, are not evidence for their claims.

Over the subsequent three weeks, I focus on two major
tasks: guiding my students through the revision assignments for their writing diagnostics and beginning the critical discussion of Mario Puzo's *The Godfather*. I assign four
revision assignments. The first is on revising introductions
(see Appendix Item 3); it requires that students produce a
clear, complete thesis, showing their reasons for their
claim and the direction of their argument. The second is
on revising overall structure (see Appendix Item 4); it requires that they outline all of their claims, indicating the
rational for the order – how each claim builds on the previous one – as well as what evidence they will use to prove
them. The third is on revising language (see Appendix Item
5); for it they must revise their introductory paragraph,
establishing clear subjects and verbs, making sentences
cohesive, and creating overall coherence. The fourth and
final revision assignment is on producing final drafts (see
Appendix Item 6); for it they must apply the skills of the
previous three assignments and write an effective conclusion. For each revision assignment we have a class discussion about the specific revision tasks. I also have my
students perform group exercises to help them start the
assignments. Each student attempts to give specific revision suggestions, based on the guidelines established
during the class discussion, to his or her partner.

The juxtaposition of guiding my students through
these revision tasks while beginning the discussion of *The
Godfather* is important pedagogically. By keeping their attention on their own analysis of the functioning of ethnic
stereotypes in *The Sopranos* while we discuss a novel that
employs such stereotypes extravagantly, I am able to keep
students from slipping back into patterns of celebration. I
focus on stereotypes as objects of power, as constructs in
the novel, steering my students away from seeing them as

markers of Italian American ethnicity. To help keep this focus, I have my students write in-class journal assignments to guide class discussions and further exercise their critical skills. These journal assignments focus on the ways in which characters adhere to or attempt to negotiate the Mafioso stereotype that is presented in the book. The journal assignments also provide material that students can use when they begin their first paper (see Appendix Item 7), which focuses on the following topic:

> In *The Godfather*, Mario Puzo presents the different cultural situations of his characters as well-defined worlds in which they live. Since these worlds are so rigidly defined, they include stereotypes, categories into which the characters sometimes fit and sometimes do not fit. In at least one case, a character tries to avoid the stereotypes by avoiding the culture itself. Michael Corleone, wanting to leave his father's world early in the novel, attempts to shift from the stereotypes that have governed his life into the separate stereotype of general American life.
>
> Though Michael is the principal character of the novel, he is not the only one who has to deal with stereotypes that are imposed on him because he is part of a specific culture. To some extent, every character in the book is doing the same thing. For this paper, you will analyze how characters succeed or fail in their negotiations of the stereotypes placed on them by cultural fellowship.

This paper assignment provides the basis for the rest of the semester. It requires the students to focus on stereotypes as forces that affect people, as constructs that people try to avoid or to use as social currency. By examining Puzo's novel, students are able to concentrate on a particular representation of these constructs. They further refine their focus by concentrating on a specific character or pair of characters from the novel. Thus, I hone their analytic skills by narrowing and simplifying the material that they must examine.

For each of the following three papers, however, I increase the complexity of the writing assignment and the corresponding critical attention that is required. For the second paper (see Appendix Item 8), they must go beyond performing a simple analysis, to the level of performing a comparative analysis, taking into account the treatments

of the Mafioso stereotype in films by Francis Ford Coppola
and Martin Scorsese. For the third paper (see Appendix
Item 9), they must evaluate a particular reaction to the
Mafioso stereotype, examining Tina De Rosa's *Paper Fish*
and determining to what level she is able to counteract
ideas of Italian Americans being associated with criminal
life. Finally, for the fourth paper (see Appendix Item 10),
they must engage in research that takes them into other
areas of the Italian American cultural experience, writing
about topics such as art, music, immigration, folklore,
and social ritual, which do not involve depictions of Mafioso culture. The papers lead my students through a deconstruction of the stereotype of the Mafioso into an exploration of some specific facet of Italian American culture
or history. This structure emphasizes the fact that only by
stripping themselves of the blinders of stereotype can they
learn about a culture.

On a basic level, I use this sequence of papers so that
in teaching my students I can meet the following goals: to
help them develop a critical awareness of the Mafioso
stereotype; to introduce them to broader, more realistic
aspects of Italian American culture; and to help them develop an ability to write increasingly sophisticated papers.
At the end of each semester I do take note of at least one
failure: at least one student wants to continue to concentrate on the stereotype, begging that he or she be allowed
to write a research paper on John Gotti, since he is a more
"interesting" Italian American subject than issues such as
folklore or immigration. This student's celebrative interest,
despite all of my efforts, is victorious in the end.

For the most part, however, students see how much
their own ideas have changed in response to their own
writing, which makes them want to learn more. I encourage this attitude by making the final class project a portfolio of all of their work. I focus on the idea that this portfolio represents a small book, one covering the Italian
American cultural experience from different perspectives.
My students must include final drafts of all of the papers,
arranged in the order in which they were written. In order
to stress the idea that they should consider each paper a
chapter in the portfolio, I have my students write a short
introduction. They must produce two paragraphs, one dis-

cussing the conclusions they reached in the first three papers, the other discussing how the research paper expanded their knowledge of Italian American life, taking them beyond the realm of the Mafioso stereotype.

On the final day of class, I have my students use this introduction to present their portfolios to their peers. By articulating the ways in which their thinking has changed as a result of their different writing projects, they learn to connect the idea of writing with an idea of growth. They learn that by setting themselves up in different critical stances towards a particular culture and the issues that surround it, they gain knowledge not only about that culture but also about their own attitudes toward it, particularly about those attitudes which previously guided their thinking without their awareness. Thus, I encourage my students to consider writing as an activity that goes beyond a specific assignment or class requirement, to being a means of learning about themselves, changing themselves, and charting their own progress.

WORKS CITED

Connors, Robert and Cheryl Glenn. *The New St. Martin's Guide to Teaching Writing*. Boston: Bedford/St. Martin's, 1999.

De Rosa, Tina. *Paper Fish*. 1980. New York: The Feminist Press at the City University of New York, 1996.

Gambino, Richard. *Blood of My Blood: The Dilemma of the Italian-Americans*. Garden City, NY: Anchor Press/Doubleday, 1975.

Hall, Stephen S. "Italian Americans: Media Perceptions." *Italian Americans: New Perspectives in Italian Immigration and Ethnicity*. Ed. Lydio F. Tomasi. New York: Center for Migration Studies of New York, 1985. 61-66.

Hendin, Josephine Gattuso. "The New World of Italian American Studies." *American Literary History* 13.1 (Spring 2001): 141-57.

Hernández, Raymond. "Congresswoman Takes a Whack at *The Sopranos* Stereotype." *New York Times* 24 May 2001, natl. ed.: B2.

Puzo, Mario. *The Godfather*. 1969. New York: Signet, 1978.

Robertson, Elizabeth and Bruce K. Martin. "Culture as Catalyst and Constraint: Toward a New Perspective on Difference." *College English* 62.4 (March 2000): 492-510.

Stenberg, Shari, and Amy Lee. "Developing Pedagogies: Learning the Teaching of English." *College English* 64.3 (January 2002): 326-47.

Story, Ralph D. "Waking Up to the World: A Multicultural Approach to Writing." *Multicultural Teaching in the University.* Ed. David Schoem et al. Westport, CT: Praeger, 1993. 191-99.

APPENDIX
SAMPLE SYLLABUS AND PAPER ASSIGNMENTS

Item 1: Syllabus

Talking with the Godfather:
Italian American Culture and the Mafia Stereotype

Required Course Texts

Aaron, Jane E. *The Little, Brown Essential Handbook for Writers.*

Williams, Joseph. *Style: Ten Lessons in Clarity and Grace.*

De Rosa, Tina. *Paper Fish.*

Puzo, Mario. *The Godfather.*

Course Description

You probably know the following story: Michael Corleone, born into a Mafia family, tries to escape his destiny, but is forced by circumstances and his own character to accept his mantle as Don. Any thought of Italian American culture calls to mind the scenario portrayed in Mario Puzo's novel and Francis Ford Coppola's film *The Godfather.* Indeed, many works by Italian American authors and artists either react to Puzo's novel and Coppola's adaptation of it or point out the cultural stereotypes that make these works so compelling to so many people. In this course, we will examine the Godfather myth and attempts by Italian Americans to explore it or overcome it.

In English 101, you learn how to write in academic, professional, and everyday situations, so that you can communicate ideas not only to teachers, but to potential employers and other people in your life. You also learn how to write about a variety of works, including literature, art, music, film, and articles.

We will cover the fundamental elements of writing, such as audience, thesis, organization, argument, and analysis. In class, we will examine how they relate to assigned readings. On an individual basis, we will apply them to student papers, which will include reviews, critical responses, analyses, and a research paper. At the end of the semester, students will have created portfolios of written work about the Italian American cultural experience. The final in-class assignment will be a presentation of the ideas contained in the portfolio.

Syllabus

Week 1   Topics: introduction and course policies; paper-writing basics; academic writing; and reading critically. Assigned reading: Raymond Hernández's "Congresswoman Takes a Whack at *The Sopranos* Stereotype." Video screening: episode of *The Sopranos*. Diagnostic writing assigned.

Week 2   Topics: discussion of ethnic stereotypes; thesis, argument, and analysis; and claims and support. In-class journal assignment #1: brainstorming for the writing diagnostic. **Due: diagnostic writing assignment.**

Week 3   Topics: discussion of diagnostics; literary interpretation; and revision tactics. Group exercises: revising introductions and refining overall structure. **Due: revised introduction to the diagnostic.**

Week 4   Topic: discussion of Mario Puzo's *The Godfather*. Assigned reading: Books I-V. In-class journal assignment #2: sons and fathers in the novel. Group exercise: revising line-by-line language. **Due: outline of revised structure for the diagnostic and revised paragraph from the diagnostic.** Paper One assigned.

Week 5   Topic: discussion of Mario Puzo's *The Godfather*. Assigned reading: Books VI-IX. In-class journal assignment #3: women in the novel. **Due: revised writing diagnostic and rough draft Pa-**

per One. Film screening: *The Godfather.* Conferences scheduled.

Week 6   Film screening: *The Godfather* (continued). Topics: discussion of Coppola's *The Godfather* and writing about film. In-class journal assignment #4: comparison of Michael Corleone in novel and film. **Due: final draft Paper One.**

Week 7   Film screening: *Goodfellas.* Paper Two assigned. Topic: discussion of film.

Week 8   Topics: discussion of film (continued) and the peer-review process. **Due: rough draft Paper Two.** Peer reviews scheduled. In-class journal assignment #5: comparison of criminal life in *The Godfather* and *Goodfellas.* Peer reviews for Paper Two.

Week 9   Topic: discussion of Tina DeRosa's *Paper Fish.* Assigned reading: pages 1-142.

Week 10   Topics: types of writing that students want to cover in the next class and the resulting discussion of these general writing topics. In-class journal assignment #6: types of writing you will need for your future. **Due: final draft Paper Two.** Paper Three assigned.

Week 11   Film screening: *Big Night.* Topic: discussion of film. **Due: rough draft Paper Three.** Peer reviews scheduled. Paper Four assigned.

Week 12   Peer reviews for Paper Three. Topic: writing research papers. Library conferences scheduled.

Week 13   Library Day. Topics: discussion of thesis issues for Paper Four; discussion of research progress; a day of Italian American music; writing about art and music; and discussion of portfolio presentations. In-class journal assignment #7: comparison of Louis Prima's "That Old Black Magic" and Frank Sinatra's "That Old Black Magic." **Due: final draft Paper Three and Paper Four**

proposals. Conferences for Paper Four proposals scheduled.

Week 14 Conferences for Paper Four proposals. End-of-semester issues. Presentation of final portfolios. Evaluations.

Item 2: Diagnostic Writing Assignment (2 to 3 pages, double-spaced)

Over the next few months we will discuss Italian American culture and the stereotypes associated with it. For the diagnostic assignment, you must join a recent debate about this issue, one focusing on how the entertainment industry portrays Italian Americans.

You have read Raymond Hernández's article, "Congresswoman Takes a Whack at *The Sopranos* Stereotype," which cites Representative Marge Roukema's criticisms of the HBO series. You have also watched *The Sopranos*, Episode 10, "A Hit Is a Hit." Respond to Roukema's criticism. You may agree or disagree with her; in fact, you may agree with some points and disagree with others. Support your opinion with specific evidence from Episode 10.

Do not panic. This is not a graded assignment. Only the revision assignments that follow will be graded. However, you should strive to do your best work on this initial draft, since stronger work now will mean stronger revisions later.

Item 3: Revision Assignment One – Introductions

Your first revision assignment is to construct a clear, complete thesis and introduction for your writing diagnostic. We discussed the differences between open, compromise, and complete theses. For this assignment, create a complete thesis. If you want to learn how to write a good open or compromise thesis, you must learn how to write a complete one.

I will grade your revision using the following guidelines:
  • To get a grade in the C range, you must indicate some opinion for which you will argue. The clearer

you make the opinion, the higher the grade you will get within the C range.

- To get a low B, you must establish a clear claim. That is, we must see not only that you have an opinion, but that it is a specific one in reference to Hernandez's article and Episode 10 of *The Sopranos*.
- To get a high B, you must set up a clear claim that indicates what you are arguing and why. You must show the reasons that you have for your claim.
- To get a grade in the A range, you must set up a clear claim, show your reasons for it, and give some idea of the direction of your argument, of what stages it will take.

For this assignment, we are not primarily concerned with line-by-line language. We will focus on that in the third revision assignment. However, if you make your language clearer you are likely to make your thoughts clearer, giving yourself a better chance of constructing a complete thesis.

Item 4: Revision Assignment Two – Structure

Now that you have revised your introduction for the writing diagnostic, you must work on the paper's overall structure. For your second revision assignment, create an outline of your new overall argument. Base this outline on your revised introduction and make it as detailed as possible. You have two major goals: to make sure that in each stage of your paper you make a clear claim that is supported by clear evidence and to make sure that each claim builds on the last, moving the argument forward.

I will grade your outline using the following guidelines:
- To get a grade in the C range, you must define each claim, showing how it relates to your new introduction and giving the evidence that supports it.
- To get a grade in the B range, you must meet the requirements for a C, plus define how each piece of evidence specifically proves each claim.
- To get a grade in the A range, you must meet all previous requirements, plus define how each claim builds on the last, drawing the reader forward.

Outline your new introduction first, giving as much clear detail as possible. Then, outline each subsequent claim. Add detail to your claims, referring to the above grading guidelines.

Item 5: Revision Assignment Three – Language

Edit your introduction using the following principles: establish clear subjects and verbs, avoid useless nominalizations, make cohesive sentences, and create overall coherence. (Remember our classroom discussion of these terms from Williams's *Style: Ten Lessons in Clarity and Grace.*) In general, strive to make the language direct and logical, so that you move from idea to idea without confusion. By doing so, you will set up the tone for the rest of your paper.

To meet the basic requirements of the assignment, you must use correct grammar. I will grade it using the following guidelines:
- To get a grade in the C range, you must establish clear subjects and verbs and avoid useless nominalizations.
- To get a grade in the B range, you must meet the requirements for a C, plus make your sentences cohesive, so that each flows from the previous one and leads to the next one.
- To get a grade in the A range, you must meet all previous requirements, plus create coherence, so that the overall topic of the passage is clear and consistent.

On the due date bring two copies of the assignment, one for me and one to use in a group exercise.

Item 6: Revision Assignment Four – Final Draft

In the previous three revision assignments, you focused on strengthening your introduction, your overall structure, and a paragraph of line-by-line language. Your final revision assignment is to apply the previous assignments to the entire paper and write a conclusion. By doing so you will produce a strong, graceful final draft.

Your conclusion must follow logically from the rest of the
paper, support the thesis, and draw together the argument. Do not leave the reader in confusion about your
stance is veer off into another idea.

The more complete you make your final draft, the higher
your grade will be. For an A, the paper must meet format-
ting guidelines, flow smoothly from idea to idea, and support each claim with concrete evidence.

Item 7: First Paper – Analysis (4-5 Pages)

Analysis of Cultural Stereotypes in Mario Puzo's *The Godfather*

Paper Topic In *The Godfather*, Mario Puzo presents the
different cultural situations of his characters as well-de-
fined worlds in which they live. Since these worlds are so
rigidly defined, they include stereotypes, categories into
which the characters sometimes fit and sometimes do not
fit. In at least one case, a character tries to avoid the stereotypes by avoiding the culture itself. Michael Corleone,
wanting to leave his father's world early in the novel, attempts to shift from the stereotypes that have governed
his life into the separate stereotype of general American
life.

Though Michael is the principal character of the novel, he
is not the only one who has to deal with stereotypes that
are imposed on him because he is part of a specific culture. To some extent, every character in the book is doing
the same thing. For this paper, you will analyze how characters succeed or fail in their negotiations of the stereotypes placed on them by cultural fellowship.

Procedure Your first task is to choose *one* of the following
approaches:
• Analyze a single character's success or lack of success
  in his or her particular cultural situation.
• Compare and contrast the success or lack of success
  of two characters who are in a similar cultural situation.

In both cases, be sure to focus on how each character either avoids or makes use of the stereotypes that are inherent to his or her culture.

In pursuing this project, try the following method. First, isolate those parts of the novel that deal with your characters and read them a couple of times, making your own notes. Second, try to answer the questions in the following "Suggested Questions" section. Third, use your notes to determine both how the character or characters succeed or fail and what traits about the character or characters seem to be responsible for this success or failure. Fourth and finally, use the ideas that you have generated to develop a working thesis and write your draft. Be discriminating. You probably will not be able to use all of your ideas. Try to decide which are most important to you.

Note: In discussing the novel, refer to it directly, using quotations and paraphrasing. You may generalize about it, but do not let your paper lapse into summary.

Suggested Questions As you think about your character or characters, ask yourself the following questions:
• What position, specifically, does the character hold within his or her culture?
• What is expected, from others within the culture, of a character in such a position?
• What is expected, from people outside the culture, of a character in such a position?
• Does the character want to hold his or her place in the culture? If not, does the character want a different place in the same culture or another culture altogether?
• If you are comparing and contrasting characters, does one fail and the other succeed? If so, how? What differences in the characters account for their different fates?
• What actions or pivotal events in the character's life determine his or her fate? In other words, what specific events add to or take away from a character's ability to fit into or negotiate the stereotypes that are expected of him or her?

Item 8: Second Paper – Comparison (5-6 Pages)

Film Depictions of Mafia Culture

Paper Topic In your first paper you analyzed specific characters within Mario Puzo's *The Godfather*, concentrating on their roles within their cultures. For your second paper, you must expand your examination of culture. You will now compare two separate artistic depictions of Mafia culture. In addition, you must now analyze a different medium, that of film.

Choose one of the following two options:
* Compare Mario Puzo's novel *The Godfather* with Francis Ford Coppola's film *The Godfather*.
* Compare Francis Ford Coppola's film *The Godfather* with Martin Scorsese's film *Goodfellas*.

An unavoidable central issue in your comparison will be the role of violence. In each of the three works in question, violence plays a major role. Ideas about Mafia culture embedded in the works are connected to their specific portrayals of violence.

Procedures To make your task easier, use the guidelines in this section to narrow your paper topic.

If you compare Puzo's novel and Coppola's film:
Choose a crucial scene or set of scenes and address how they are presented in each work. Discuss the choices that the filmmaker makes in transforming the novel's story into his own, separate medium of expression. Discuss, as well, the different impacts – emotional, intellectual, and otherwise – that the scenes have. Does the director sacrifice a certain intellectual impact in order to heighten an emotional impact, or is it the other way around? What different views of the Mafia culture do these different representations give? Does the director change the time involved or the sequence of events? What does the director leave out? What does he add? Why do these omissions or additions matter, in terms of the portrayal of culture in each work?

If you compare Coppola's film and Scorsese's film:

Define, in both cases, the central character's role in Mafia culture. As part of this definition, discuss the structure of that culture. How does the character enter the culture? What status does the character have outside the culture? Does the character remain in the culture? How do the different representations of Mafia culture and the different representations of the characters' reactions to it reflect on common ideas about the larger Italian American culture? Do we, as viewers, have the same attitudes towards the Mafia cultures presented in the films that the characters do? Are our attitudes different? If so, what effect do these differences have on our involvement with the central characters?

After you use these questions to generate ideas, remember to narrow them to a particular claim, a precise thesis that you want to prove. Use this thesis to focus your paper.

Item 9: Third Paper – Evaluation (5-7 Pages)

Choosing an Italian American Family

Paper Topic In "A Song from the Ghetto," the afterword to Tina De Rosa's *Paper Fish*, Edvige Giunta speaks out against "Popular cultural representations of Italians...[which] have focused on the mafia wars and on such notorious figures as Al Capone. These figures, like Mario Puzo's and Francis Ford Coppola's Don Vito Corleone, appeal to the fantastic vision of Italians that mainstream American has cultivated..." (138). Giunta goes on to present the idea that De Rosa writes her novel in response to such representations, that she defies "stereotypical representations of Chicago Italian Americans as mobsters by portraying the very neighborhood ruled by Al Capone in a completely different light..." (138). Thus, De Rosa, to some extent, sets her family in fiction against the fictional family of the Corleones.

Your task in this paper is to evaluate De Rosa's depiction. Ultimately, your paper must address the following topic: whether De Rosa, in setting herself against stereotypical representations of Italian Americans, counteracts these representations or merely sets up another set of stereotypes that, while different, include their own problems. That is, does De Rosa negate the Godfather image, or does she set up another image that is just as stereotypical?

The Elements of an Evaluation In your evaluation, you must do the following:

1. Identify the criteria of evaluation. Assuming that De Rosa's purpose is to counteract existing stereotypical views of Italian Americans, you must decide what someone would have to do to achieve such a purpose. What elements are necessary in a work of fiction that is meant to topple the stereotype of Italian Americans as gangsters?
2. Show how De Rosa does or does not meet these criteria. By doing so, you determine whether or not De Rosa fulfills at least one of her purposes in writing her novel.

Narrowing the Topic To determine your criteria for evaluation and thereby develop your thesis for the paper, consider the following questions:

- In *The Godfather*, Puzo sets up the image of the Godfather as the defining archetype of the novel, the figure by which we must judge all other figures. What archetype or archetypes does De Rosa set up in *Paper Fish*? Are the characters who must define themselves in response to these archetypes in better or worse positions than the characters in *The Godfather*?
- What is the scope of the novel? That is, how much of the Italian American world does it seek to portray? What are the cultural positions of the characters within the novel? Does this affect our assessment of it as counteracting stereotypes of Italian Americans? If so, how?
- Is the fragmented structure of the novel related to De Rosa's project of overcoming prevailing stereotypes of Italian Americans? If so, how?
- Which novel, *Paper Fish* or *The Godfather*, seems to place Italian Americans more in the mainstream of American culture? In doing so, does the novel add to or subtract from stereotypical representations of Italian Americans?

- Would it be preferable to grow up in the BellaCasa family or the Corleone family? Why?

Since this paper is an evaluation, it openly demands an opinion on the writer's part. The trick is to make that opinion count, to make the reader feel that it is not merely an opinion, but a reasoned response to De Rosa's project. For this reason, all of the issues regarding thesis and evidence that we have discussed over the course of the semester become even more crucial. Try to give your paper the status of an objective evaluation, rather than a personal reaction.

Item 10: Fourth Paper – Research (8-10 Pages)

Explorations in the Italian American Cultural Experience

Paper Topic Over the course of the semester, you have written about the Godfather stereotype and responses to it in Italian American culture. Also, you have written papers based on focused assignments, so that your choice of topic was limited. For this paper, you have a chance to expand the field, to explore other aspects of Italian American life as well as discuss a topic of particular interest to you.

Note: Though you may choose your topic from a broad arena, you must ensure that your topic itself is not broad. That is, your topic must be more focused than "Italian American life in general." You must choose some aspect or category of Italian American life, then ask questions about it until you develop a thesis to pursue.

You may choose one of the following categories: the impact of a specific Italian American person; works of art or music by Italian Americans; the Italian American immigrant experience; or Italian American folklore and social ritual. Once you have begun your research, you may find that your discussion actually spans more than one topic. However, you must begin by limiting the field. Remember, you must find a topic within one of the categories, then develop a thesis within that topic.

The Impact of a Specific Italian American
In this category, you have a wealth of choices. Examples include, *but are not limited to,* the following: in the area of science, Enrico Fermi, the nuclear physicist; in politics, Fiorello LaGuardia, the reformer and mayor of New York in the 1930s and 1940s, or Nicola Sacco and Bartolomeo Vanzetti, the anarchists whose execution drew national attention and spawned national controversy; in music, singers and musicians such as Louis Prima and Frank Sinatra; in sports, the catcher Yogi Berra; and in film, actors such as Rudolf Valentino and Anne Bancroft or a director such as Frank Capra. Choose a figure, then ask questions. What effect did he or she have on American life? What effect did it have on him or her? Was he or she an immigrant or born here? What impact did Italian heritage have on his or her role in the American scene? Keep asking questions and limiting your topic until you have discovered two or three particularities or characteristics about the person that you can use to develop a thesis.

Art or Music by Italian Americans
Choose a work or works of art or music by Italian Americans. If you choose more than one work of art or music, they must be linked by either similarities or differences that you can discuss. Concentrate on how the work was produced, the context in which it was generated, as well as responses to it. From this discussion, try to discover the larger meanings or contexts of the work. What about it is particularly Italian? What is American? How do the two aspects blend?

The Italian American Immigrant Experience
Discuss some aspect of Italian American migration patterns or settlement. You might try examining a particular Italian American neighborhood or set of neighborhoods. What determines the formations of these neighborhoods? How much is based on exclusion by existing natives and how much is based on choices by the immigrant such as the availability of work or a preference to be around people from a specific region of Italy? What is the history of the neighborhood? How does it change over time and why?

Italian American Folklore and Social Ritual

Examine an Italian American social structure or custom. Areas include the following: the Italian American family system; ideas about birth, health, and death; weddings or other religious ceremonies; a holiday such as St. Joseph's Day and the customs surrounding it; Italian American stories and storytelling; supernaturalism and supernatural practices, such as the *malocchio* (the evil-eye); aspects of language such as the influence of Italian on English and vice versa or the lingering influence of Italian proverbs in Italian American life; and the role of food in Italian American life or the interaction of Italian and American cuisine.

WARNING Begin thinking about this paper right away. You have some time before your proposal is due, but you should begin researching and writing as soon as possible. If you wish, make an appointment with me to discuss your ideas and your overall thesis. We will discuss your topic and possible sources related to it on our Library Research day. It is in your best interest to begin talking with me about your ideas before you turn in your proposal.

Proposal Your proposal should be typed, and should include your name, the date, and page numbers. It should consist of the following sections:
1. A brief statement (one to three sentences) of your working thesis.
2. A rough draft of your first paragraph, incorporating or reflecting your working thesis.
3. A rough summary or outline of the issues you plan to touch on in your discussion.

An annotated bibliography showing me that you have begun research and that you have some idea of the material at your disposal. Your research paper requires four sources. As you write, you will probably weed out sources that you initially think are useful, so include six to eight in your annotated bibliography.

Luciano Bianciardi's *Viaggio in Barberia* and the Reconstruction of Memory

Mark Pietralunga
FLORIDA STATE UNIVERSITY

"Why Expeditionaries?" This is the question Eric Leed poses in the introductory chapter to his book, *Shores of Discovery. How Expeditionaries Have Constructed the World*, in which he explores the different forms of expeditions and their purposes, the relations that they embody, as well as those that they create between peoples. Leed begins his study by stating that *expedition* "means nothing less than a 'walking out,' egressing familiar country into unknown territory" (3). In reviewing the lives and travels of numerous expeditionaries, Leed observes that many expeditions set out to recover someone or something lost. Additionally, he argues that recovery is both a motive of many epic journeys as well as a feature of historical expeditions. Much like Leed, Luciano Bianciardi recognizes that in the apparent simplicity of terms like *expedition* and *viaggio* there lies a variety of meanings and relations. In the article, "Libri di viaggio e guide di tutti i tempi," Bianciardi offers examples that illustrate the richness and diversity of traveling:

> Yuri Gargarin stupisce il mondo con il suo viaggio spazziale [...] Viaggiatori per definizione furono Colombo, Magellano e Marco Polo: li spingeva – almeno i primi due – il solo desiderio di conoscere altre terre, di allargare i confini del mondo accessibile all'uomo [...] Ci sono stati viaggiatori come Paolo di Tarso, spinti dalla luce folgorante della parola divina [...] e ci sono stati viaggiatori come Francesco Pizarro, spinti dalla brama di portare la 'civiltà' a chi già una civiltà aveva, splendida ma disarmata [...] Si è viaggiato e si viaggia mossi dalla pietà, e in tal caso siamo pellegrini o 'romei.' Due secoli or sono un nobiluomo inglese non si reputava tale se non aveva prima compiuto il suo 'grand tour,' il viaggio cioè ai paesi caldi e ricchi d'arte, giù oltre le Alpi, fino a Roma e poi a Napoli [...] Persino il cosiddetto 'week end,' persino la scampagnata, sono viaggio. Persino chi esce la sera a fare 'un giretto' (magari col cagnolino dietro) fa un suo piccolissimo, ma non disonorevole, viaggio; e si sono fatti 'viaggi in

libreria' e 'giri della propria camera': anche in questo caso si è sempre finito per scoprire qualcosa. (989)

Notwithstanding his fascination with the sense of discovery implicit in the act of traveling, Bianciardi's writings also reveal both an ideological and physiological resistance to travel.[1] Bianciardi's love/hate relationship with travel finds its best expression in the diary of his trip to North Africa in 1968, *Viaggio in Barberia*.[2] The volume begins with Bianciardi attempting to understand "l'ipotesi lavorativa" of those who had decided on and proposed this *expedition* to North Africa. Such reflections prompt the following unheroic self-portrait of the author as traveler:

---

[1] In his novel *La vita agra*, Bianciardi's protagonist appears to express the author's views on the futilty and limitations of travel: "E poi viaggiare secondo me non serve a nulla, ai giorni nostri, non ci impari proprio niente. Anche uno che abbia ambizione di scrivere, non è che viaggiando apprenda qualcosa di nuovo, o trovi argomenti da raccontare. Al massimo potrà scrivere qualche articolo di giornale, ma se è una persona seria, tornando si guarda bene dal mettere sulla carta quello che ha visto, o creduto di vedere. Io per esempio ho un amico scrittore, che una volta andò in aereo sino a Pechino, nel Catai, come dicevano gli antichi. Eppure, siccome è uno scrittore serio, tornando non si è mica messo a parlare dei cinesi! Al contrario, ha continuato a parlare dei cecinesi, e fa bene, perchè quelli li conosce davvero" (189).

[2] In the volume, *Carte su carte di ribaltura: Luciano Bianciardi Traduttore*, Maria Stella offers an insightful commentary on Bianciardi's ambiguous relationship with travel: "Io credo che il rapporto di Bianciardi con il viaggio sia essenzialmente un rapporto di odio/amore. Da una parte infatti c'è il Bianciardi anarchico che rifiuta la massificazione del viaggio contemporaneo, viaggio che finisce per essere parte del boom economico e manualistico di quegli anni, per creare quello che si può definire il "mito dell'evasione," ed è facile qui pensare alla pubblicistica proprio di guide di viaggio. Bianciardi è molto critico sui desideri di allontanamento dalla realtà, perché scrive più volte che la realtà si vive, si affronta, si conosce essendo profondamente presenti ad essa, e non fuggendola. D'altra parte c'è una nozione di viaggio come ricerca, come conoscenza, come metodo di messa in crisi di una realtà e di una cultura, il viaggio che ci permette di guardarci dall'esterno con occhio critico e diverso da quello abituale: ed ecco Bianciardi che attraversa il Maghreb e che medita su questa esperienza totale che mette in discussione il suo intero essere e che egli analizza in un libro straordinario come *Viaggio in Barberia*" (150-51).

A quarantacinque anni suonati io non ho mai imparato come funzioni un motore a scoppio, non ho la patente, non so guidare, nutro una spiccata, allegra ma feroce avversione verso i feticisti dell'automobile, fustigo i primatisti del 'da casello a casello' e vado in bicicletta. A tempo perso suono il violoncello e mi guadagno da vivere con le parole che scrivo. Voglio dire, sono un sedentario, un abitudinario e l'idea di una partenza mattutina mi dà l'insonnia. (1)

Bianciardi had already expressed his opinion about man and the automobile in his 1962 best-selling novel, *La vita agra,* a satiric dirge to city life in the Italy of the so-called "miracle years." In a 1963 radio broadcast entitled "L'uomo e la macchina nella società industriale," conducted by sociologist Franco Ferrarotti, Bianciardi recalls a passage from his novel in which he treats the relationship between man and machine in modern society. Bianciardi observes:

Nel mio libro, verso la fine, c'è un personaggio, il protagonista, che sogna, anzi delira, di un mondo da cui siano scomparse le macchine, un mondo in cui le automobili vengono abbandonate per via ai giochi dei bimbi, ai quali nessuno tuttavia dovrà dire a che cosa servivano un tempo; un mondo in cui la produzione industriale sia terminata, in cui non esistono più bisogni, in cui la gente viva solo di agricoltura e soprattutto di amore. Io credo in quel sogno, credo in quel delirio? Ecco, direi, che quando noi sognamo, noi tutti, l'età dell'oro non ce la configuriamo affatto come un'età senza macchine; è semmai un'età in cui le macchine venivano usate meglio, perché tutta la storia dell'uomo, tutta la storia della civiltà, è una storia d'invenzione, di macchine! [...] Va condannata semmai la falsatura per cui la macchina non è più uno strumento che ci libera, ma diventa un fine essa stessa; la falsatura per cui la macchina non serve più a noi, ma siamo noi che serviamo la macchina. (261)

While recognizing the hyperbolic nature of such fantasies as those in which machines have been abandoned, Bianciardi insists on their utility. Such fantasies are a reminder that in the world of mass consumption and mass production it is man who is at the service of the objects and machines; instead, it ought to be the individual who makes this choice. Similarly, the dream of a small earthly paradise in which men have been transformed into children is a reminder that there is much to learn from one's past. For Bianciardi, in today's world the new city no longer looks to the past, as it once did; instead, it looks only to the future. Today's cities have broken with the past, the golden age is no longer behind us. Man looks only ahead as the world moves forward. Taking into consideration this perspective, Bianciardi's *Viaggio in Barberia* becomes much more than the simple geographical displacement of a reluctant traveler, who sets out with his four traveling companions on a 8000 mile expedition across North Africa in a 125 Fiat to write a travel piece sponsored, ironically, by a magazine for automotive enthusiasts, "L'Automobile," and Fiat, the automobile manufacturing giant. The sedentary Bianciardi discovers a sense of freedom in this world of the itinerant man, which, in turn, enables him to recover something lost.

In his study *The Mind of the Traveler*, Eric Leed distinguishes philosophical travel from other forms of travel. He writes: "Philosophical travel is travel in time, a journey to the sites of the beginnings of one's cultural order. As a search for roots and beginnings, philosophical travel might equally be called 'historical travel,' for in this sort of journey the traveler attempts to retrace the paths of one's ancestors or one's own past" (133). Leed goes on to point out that there is clearly "a fine line between philosophical travel and ritual journeys to reaffirm identities" (133). As a result, geographical displacement coincides with a chronological displacement. Additionally, Leed suggests that "travel and departure are often regarded as a purge, a stripping of the accommodated self, which might improve and clarify a person's outlines" (46-47). As Bianciardi prepares his trip to North Africa, he comes to realize that certain commodities associated with his everyday chaotic life as a translator/writer/journalist as well as those products indicative of someone allergic to traveling are no longer of use to him: "Inutile la macchina per scrivere, inutile il mio bel binocolo da campagna, inutile l'intera borsa di medicinali – sieri contro la vipera e contro lo scorpione, potabilizzatori dell'acqua, lacci emostatici, panetti d'allume di rocca, bende garze filacce" (2-3). Instead, what proves most valuable to Bianciardi in this journey is his memory. It is through memory that the journey becomes a rejuvenating experience. From the opening lines of *Viaggio in Barberia,* Bianciardi's trip to the Maghreb region becomes closely linked to the author's past, most notably to his childhood . However, it is only midway through the journey that the author, after a series of encounters that are a reminder of his youth, begins to appreciate fully the connection between the trip and his childhood: "E cominciamo a capire che questa scorribanda in Barberia è anche un viaggio nella memoria. Cioè nell'infanzia" (64).

Before his departure, Bianciardi, like most travelers, eagerly seeks to acquaint himself with the Maghreb region's history, its geography, and its people. Bianciardi's familiarity with this region is limited to a chaotic mixture of notions learned at school, clichès, and heresay. One recollection is particularly noteworthy in our attempt to understand this trip to North Africa as journey to one's childhood. It is the memory of a street in his hometown of Grosseto named "via dei Barberi." Bianciardi writes: "A Grosseto esisteva, ed esiste ancora, una via dei Barberi, e faceva angolo con la via del Saracino, in fondo alla quale sorgevano i due villini, rosa e azzurro, oggi trasformati in casa di civile abitazione, assai esposta alle piene dell'Ombrone.[3] 'Che, vai in via dei Barberi?" ci chiedevammo ammiccando" (3). The strong connection between the journey to his childhood and the trip to North Africa is further solidified at the moment he leaves Italian soil. At this point, Bianciardi senses a type of liberation of the obsessions and fears associated to life in the present: "E non appena le ruote si furono staccate dal cemento di Fiumicino, mi caddero di dosso, come d'incanto, le paure: non sognai più il salotto buono della signora potentissima, dimenticai le fosche profezie dello Scacchigracco [...] Come ai tempi della mia adolescenza (m'ero alterato la carta d'identità) ormai stavo per imboccare la via dei Barberi" (8).

The journey begins in Tripoli, a city that evokes a series of associations with familiar places in the minds of the four adult travelers:

---

[3] Grosseto is situated at the mouth of the Ombrone river.

> Nel buio si capiva poco che cosa fosse Tripoli: pareva una fila
> di casette intervallate da qualche stenta pianta e da qualche
> mucchio di terra, forse ghiaia, forse polvere, forse sabbia,
> chissà. Si sa invece che la mente adulta è pigra e ragiona per
> confronti. Attaccò Maria: 'Mi pare Ostia nel trenta.' Concordo
> sulla data, ma non sul luogo: 'Più che Ostia direi San Rocco,
> quella che oggi si chiama Marina di Grosseto. Di là dal
> fossino è ancora così.' Poi ci ripenso e dico no, questa è
> Ribolla. (10)

For Bianciardi, the adult travelers are more relativistic in
their attempt to find sources of orientation. This behavior
reflects a mentality that is more adaptive than creative.[4]
Gaia De Pascale has observed that the only traveler who is
able to reason in dialectic terms is Marcellino, Bianciardi's
ten-year old son. Recalling the words of Baudelaire, De
Pascale distinguishes the vast universe of the child from
the more restricted sphere of the adults: "Del resto 'Pour
l'enfant, amoureux de cartes et d'estampes,/ L'univers est
égal à son vaste appétit,' mentre agli occhi dell'adulto che
molto ha già visto, il mondo risulta 'monotone et petit' "
(124).

In the town of Mahdia, along the coast of Tunisia,
Bianciardi and his fellow travelling companions are
amazed to see how the locals tolerate the presence of an
inordinate number of flies. This experience leads Bianciardi to the question: "Ma quand'è che abbiamo smesso,
noi europei, di sopportare le mosche?" (22) Bianciardi's
query enables him to return once again to his childhood:

> Dopo tutto dovremmo rammentarla, la nostra infanzia: la
> carta moschicida, quell'ignobile lista appesa al centro del

---

[4] The epilogue to Eric Leed's *The Mind of the Traveler* addresses the
relationship of the modern mind of the traveler with the experience of
travel. With regard to modern travel's apparent lack of heroic and
individualizing qualities, Leed writes: "Perhaps this is only to say that
our time is the bitter end of the dialectic, and a time of sorrow for those
who have defined their identities in terms of outer and opposing worlds
of others. Those oppositions that once operated between civility and a
surrounding antithesis of the wilderness are now boundaries within. The
dialectic has been internalized and is a structual element within the
society of travelers" (288).

soffitto, nera d'insetti appiccicati. L'odore acre e disgustoso del flit. Le stalle verniciate di azzurro [...] La guerra contro le mosche. Vincevano sempre le mosche. Il tafano, detto anche mosca cavallina. In greco "assillo." Donde il verbo assillare, che equivale paro paro al toscano tafanare. Smettetela di tafanare [...] Da bambino me ne entrò uno in un orecchio. A scuola, per distrarci, acchiappavamo le mosche. E allora, perché non le sopportiamo più? La risposta è: DDT. La data, il '46. Dunque, ventidue anni che non tolleriamo più le mosche, le abbiamo escluse dalla nostra vita quotidiana, e anche dalla nostra cultura. Non possiamo più parlare di mosca cocchiera. Non possiamo più dire zitto e mosca. La sambuca con la mosca comincia a suonare arbitrio [...]. (22)

Such reflections prompt Bianciardi to do a rapid mental entomological review, which results in the conviction that nearly all insects have been excluded from our daily habitat:

Non so da quanto tempo non vedo più un grillo nè un grillo moro come quelli fiorentini il giorno dell'Assunzione, nè grilli canterini come quelli nostrani. I quali non cantavano, se ben rammento, ma semmai suonavano. Strofinandosi le ali sul corpo. Non vedo più formiche, e nessuno dei presenti sa dirmi il preciso signficato della parola *cudera* [...] Non vedo da anni libellule, che noi ragazzini chiamavano "cavaocchi" convinti sul serio che volessero e potessero cavare gli occhi a qualcuno [...] Non so di preciso cosa sia la filossera. Mi dicono che gli anticrittogamici ne han fatto sterminio. Ne abbiamo spopolato i campi. Abbiamo, ovviamente, tolto il cibo agli uccelli che difatti scarseggiano, e non soltanto per la protervia dei nostri cacciatori. Insomma, ci stiamo preparando a vivere in un mondo privo di insetti. Non tolleriamo le pulci neanche addosso al cane, il quale forse con le pulci vive bene, se notiamo la voluttà con cui si gratta. Male, molto male, un mondo senza insetti, è una dimensione di vita che ci viene meno. (22-23)

Bianciardi's query and reflections anticipate Pasolini's reference to the disappearance of fireflies, a poetic image of an Italy that, in many ways, was changing for the worse in the post-war years (most notably during the "miracle" years): an Italy where old values, dialects and traditions were about to be destroyed forever: Pasolini writes: "Nei primi anni sessanta a causa dell'inquinamento dell'aria, e,

soprattutto, in campagna, a causa dell'inquinamento dell'-
acqua (gli azzurri fiumi e le rogge trasparenti) sono comin-
ciate a scomparire le lucciole. Il fenomeno è stato fulmineo
e folgorante. Dopo pochi anni le lucciole non c'erano più.
(Sono ora un ricordo, abbastanza straziante, del passato: e
un uomo anziano che abbia un tale ricordo, non può
riconoscere nei nuovi giovani se stesso giovane, e dunque
non può più avere i bei rimpianti di una volta.)" (129).
Pasolini's essay ends with the following nostalgic wish: "Ad
ogni modo, quanto a me (se ciò ha qualche interesse per il
lettore) sia chiaro: io, ancorché multinazionale, darei
l'intera Montedison per una lucciola" (134). In this light, it
is appropriate to recall that the protagonist of Bianciardi's
novel, *La vita agra*, who is a self-proclaimed anarchist, has
come to Milan from the provinces to execute a hostile mis-
sion against another industrial conglomerate, Montecatini,
which he considered responsible for the death of forty-
three miners in a mine explosion near his hometown of
Grosseto in 1954.[5] Through this action, the young intellectual from the provinces intends to vindicate those
miners who had lost their lives as a result of a company
that allowed industrial and commercial interests to prevail

---

[5] See Bianciardi and Cassola's *I minatori della Maremma*. In this
sociological inquiry on the living and working conditions in the mines of
the Maremma region, the authors investigate the tragic explosion of May
1954 in the mine at Ribolla and denounce those responsible for the
death of the forty-three mine workers. Additionally, in his essay "Lettera
a Milano," Bianciardi explains those reasons that prompted him to move
from the provinces to Milan: "Perciò, quando mi proposero di venire
quassù [Milan], io mi chiesi se era giusto lasciare i badilanti e i minatori,
della cui vicinanza sentivo molto il bisogno e il signficato. Non solo:
pensai anche che la lotta, quassù, si poteva condurre con mezzi migliori,
più affinati, e a contatto diretto con il nemico. Mi pareva anzi che
quassù, il nemico dovesse presentarsi più scoperto e visibile. A Niccioleta
la Montecatini non ha altra faccia se non quella delle guardie giurate,
povera gente che cerca di campare, o quella del direttore, un ragazzo
della mia età, potrebbe aver fatto con me il liceo, o giocato a pallone. A
Milano invece la Montecatini è quei due palazzoni di marmo, vetro e
alluminio, dieci, dodici piani, all'angolo fra via Turati e via della Moscova.
A Milano la Montecatini ha il cervello, quindi dobbiamo anche noi
spostare il nostro cervello quassù, e cercare di migliorarlo, di farlo
funzionare nella maniera e nella direzione giusta. Così ragionavo, e per
questo mi decisi" (220).

over human welfare. For Bianciardi, the appearance of DDT signaled the arrival of homogenizing cultural imports that placed local populations on the defensive and opened the way to their integration into a consumer market. A primary consequence of this homogenization of culture at the hands of progress is a loss of our linguistic identity.[6] The richness associated with the cultural and linguistic diversity from region to region constitutes, for both Bianciardi and Pasolini, a patrimony that cannot be lost, degraded, or homogenized, for the simple fact that it forms a rich reservoir capable of nourishing the ideas as well as the needs of an entire nation.

Bianciardi's *La vita agra* is a novel of protest against the so-called miracle taking place in Milan and the angry statement of his failure to defeat it. Both the protest and failure are depicted by the protagonist's attempt to undermine the capitalistic system that ultimately consumes him. In his journey through North Africa, there are several instances in which Bianciardi is reminded of his succumbing to progress and his integration into consumer society. One such instance occurs as Bianciardi and his fellow travellers approach cities in Tunisia and Algiers and, as Europeans, find comfort at the appearance of the inescapable signs of modernity, which are especially evident in these North African countries undergoing a process of transformation: "Finalmente!' 'Ma cosa finalmente?' 'Ma la ciminiere! Un cementificio, le citroen, un

---

[6] For Bianciardi and Pasolini, the impact of mass-media in the 'miracle years' resulted in the disappearance of an autonomous popular world identified with a variety of local dialects and traditions. With specific reference to the leveling of the Italian language, Bianciardi writes: "È ormai abbastanza ovvio quel che si va ripetendo da più parti: la televisione, in Italia, sta facendo l'unità linguistica. Un paese fortemente diviso, trova tuttavia e – magari suo malgrado – un proprio comune denominatore fonetico, sintattico, grammaticale" ("Nasce una nuova lingua," 8). Similarly, Pasolini observes: "La presenza del 'principio tecnologico', come principio omologatore e modificatore, e quindi nazionalizzatore dell'italiano, mi si è rivelata attraverso la sua azione – iniziale, ma già aberrante e patologica – sui vari tipi di linguaggio: che appunto, mi sono apparsi tutti 'negativi': il linguaggio del giornalismo, della televisione, della pubblicità, della politica, del parlar comune del Nord, ecc." ("Diario linguistico" 95).

grattacielo? Finalmente!' Tu credi, europeo marcio, di amare il deserto, la natura, la campagna, ma poi dici 'finalmente' quando ricompaiono i segni dell'odiata civiltà. Proprio così, ogni volta che trovi una grande città, lì sei a casa tua. *Ubi domus ibi patria*, specialmente se la *domus* è un albergo chiamato Claridge e arredato all'inglese, con vetrinette e poltroncine" (25). Eric Leed suggests that in modern journeys "the would-be individual, defined by modern circumstance, often learns that modernity is inescapable, that there is no longer a boundary between the civilized and the uncivilized" (*The Mind of the Traveler* 50). Bianciardi's encounter with modernity in North Africa only emphasizes his need for escape and self-definition through detachments from the familiar, from those aspects of the modern civilization with which, he, as a "europeo marcio," has become obsessed. The arrival in the Algerian town of Palestro appears to offer Bianciardi the opportunity to return to the beginnings of his cultural order and to the foundational myths of his childhood. Palestro inspires in Bianciardi the memory of an important Franco-Piedmontese victory against the Austrians during the Risorgimento (May 1859). Bianciardi's biographer, Pino Corrias, helps us to understand the significance of the Risorgimento to the writer and the connection of this moment in history with his childhood:

> Condividono [Bianciardi and his father] due passioni: il calcio [...] e il Risorgimento. È lui [his father] che regala al figlio, ottavo compleanno, *I Mille* di Giuseppe Bandi, garibaldino [...] è anche il libro che gli darà spunto per scrivere *La battaglia soda, Aprire il fuoco, Garibaldi*, quello che gli regalerà una passione perpetua che nessuno, su a Milano, capiva. Una sera degli anni Sessanta, Giovanni Arpino [...] gli dirà: 'Ma si può sapere cosa te ne frega a te di Garibaldi?' Non poteva sapere che per Bianciardi il Risorgimento era soprattutto un legame con la sua infanzia, un ricordarsi per sempre ragazzino grossetano che rilegge le stesse pagine, la stessa storia, e sogna i garibaldini nella cameretta di casa, finestra aperta e sussidiario chiuso [...]. (31-32)

In his popularized historical study of the Risorgimento, *Daghela avanti un passo!,"* written in 1969 and originally intended for a young audience of readers, Bianciardi sum-

marizes the events of the Franco-Austrian war, or the second war of Italian Unification, in upper Lombardy surrounding the battle of Palestro. Bianciardi's description of
Napoleon III's casualties allows us to appreciate the Algerian connection with the Risorgimento and the reason
for the author's full attention as the band of travelers is
about to arrive in the town of Palestro:

> Frattanto Napoleone III se ne tornava a casa sua. Ma
> lasciava in Italia duemila morti. I loro nomi scritti, dal primo
> all'ultimo, sul piedistallo del monumento che all'imperatore
> eressero i milanesi. Li possiamo leggere ancora, al parco:
> quattro generali, una decina di colonnelli, una trentina di
> altri ufficiali, centinaia di umili soldati. Non tutti si
> chiamano, di nome, Jean, o Pierre, o Auguste. No, ce ne sono
> di quelli, e non pochi, che si chaimano Alì, Mohammed,
> Gamal. Tutti nati in Algeria: costituivano i reparti di prima
> schiera, e venivano chiamati gli zuavi. È bene rammentar-
> selo: all'unità d'Italia hanno contribuito anche loro. (77-78)

Upon arrival in the much anticipated town, Bianciardi is
met with disappointment when he learns that its name
has been changed from Palestro to Lathdaria: "Ma è per
me una grossa delusione, perché la benzina c'è, a Palestro,
ma non c'è più Palestro, che ha cambiato nome. Si chiama
Lathdaria, ed è un vero peccato, anzi un'ingiustizia, perché a Palestro si batterono gli zuavi, che eran come si è
detto algerini" (39). As Bianciardi attempts to narrate the
Algerian ties with the Risorgimento, he quickly learns that
the Algerian youngsters are no different from their con-
temporaries in Italy: "Cerco di spiegarlo al giovanotto della
pompa, ma mi accorgo che non gliene importa nulla. Ah,
questi ragazzi di oggi, come curano poco la storia del
Risorgimento" (39-40). For Bianciardi, this lack of interest
in history is one more sign that old values and traditions
have disappeared, only to be supplanted by a consumer
identity that is not historically founded. Bianciardi's exchange with the youth recalls Pasolini's above-mentioned
nostalgic words regarding the memories of the vanished
fireflies: "un uomo anziano che abbia un tale ricordo, non

può riconoscere nei nuovi giovani se stesso giovane, e dunque non può più avere i bei rimpianti di una volta."[7] Notwithstanding this disconnect with the Algerian youth, Bianciardi, nevertheless, returns to memories of his own childhood to find a connection with this land and its people: "Così, all'improvviso, salta fuori l'ultimo nesso, dimenticato, fra me e la Barberia. Nonna Albina. Morì che io avevo sette anni, ma rammento che ogni volta, incontrandomi, mi pagava da bere un tamarindo e mi ripeteva che giù a Fez noi dovevamo incassare un'eredità [...] Non a caso nonna Albina era alta e mora, mora mia madre, mori tutti i miei zii, e sono moro anch'io" (4). While Bianciardi's childlike treasure hunt for his inheritance in the Moroccan town of Fez proves to be fruitless, this search reveals a need to identify with the African people. A brief reference to Bianciardi's final novel, *Aprire il fuoco,* helps us to ascertain this identification with the North Africans. In the novel, the historical event of the "Cinque Giornate" is set in contemporary 1959 Italy and is viewed as a "rivoluzione che andò fallita."[8] The protagonist of the novel is a revolutionary professor who has been exiled from Milan and who finds refuge in the seaside town of Nesci.[9] From his exile, the protagonist, having been deprived of a cause, sees no values in which to believe. The fact that he sees himself as a permanent "inquilino" confirms his sense of alienation and a feeling of not belonging. Having failed to re-ignite the mythical passions of the past, his only solution is death. In the concluding lines of the novel, the

[7] See Bianciardi's article, "E dunque, che lingua fa," in which the author examines how the linguistic changes due in large part to the mass-media culture have resulted in the loss of common points of reference between generations.
[8] Bianciardi's description recalls Antonio Gramsci's views of the Risorgimento as a "rivoluzione mancata" rejecting, writes Lucy Riall, the "national explanation of unification, pointing instead to the persistence of regional and local identities/conflicts in Risorgimento Italy" (65).
[9] Nesci is the fictitious name for the seaside town of Rapallo. Zolita Louise Vella notes that Nesci is a "play on the Latin verb 'nescio': to know not, to ignore, and a commonly used word in the Ligurian dialect that means idiot, stupid, ignorant" (154).

protagonist's delirious nightmare not only forecasts his death but it also emphasizes his diversity:

> L'altra notte mi destai di soprassalto ed ero in una corsia dell'ospedale di Capetown. Letti di qua e letti di là, con tutta la gente nera che spiccava sul bianco delle lenzuola. Chino su di me, in camice verdino, un uomo alto e biondo che mostrava i denti all'infermiera [...] 'Eletttroencefalogramma piatto. Clinicamente tu sei morto. Vuoi insegnare il mestiere a me? Il cervello non ti funziona più. Possiamo procedere.' Mi aggrappai come un disperato all'ultima speranza, e giuravo che non era quello il posto mio, che non dovevo trovarmi lì in corsia fra i negri. Cittadinanza italiana, giuravo, razza bianca. Avete visto il passaporto. 'Abbiamo visto, abbiamo visto, la tua faccia di beduino. E la storia della bella Marisilia, allora?" sogghignò l'uomo coi denti. "C'è di sicuro un ascendente femminile di razza nera. Possiamo procedere." Io scongiurai ancora, cavillando, dissi che i beduini non sono negri, che la negritudine comincia dai tropici, ma quello continuava a crollare il capo ghignando con tutti quei denti. 'La negritudine comincia dall' Ombrone.'[10] E mi venne il sonno, per sempre. (191-92)

Maria Clotilde Angelini has noted how Bianciardi's identification with negritude underlines his feeling of diversity and separation. Additionally, Angelini reminds us that some years earlier Bianciardi had already written of his inherent incapacity to resemble the Milanese "formiche" and of the suspicion and distrust he had encountered in the North "per quel razzismo antimeridionale che in *Aprire il fuoco* è portato sino alla identificazione di non settentrionale = negro e pertanto 'escluso' a vita" (109).[11] The

---

[10] See note 3.

[11] In the following passage from *La vita agra*, Bianciardi's protagonist decribes his struggles in the Northern Italian metropolis: "Quassù io ero venuto non per far crescere le medie e i bisogni, ma per distruggere il torracchione di vetro e cemento, con tutte le umane relazioni che ci stanno dentro ... E se ora ritorno al mio paese, e ci incontro Tacconi Otello, che cosa gli dico? [...] Posso, dirgli, guarda, Tacconi, lassù mi hanno ridotto che a fatica mi difendo, lassù se caschi per terra nessuno ti raccatta, e la forza che ho mi basta appena per non farmi mangiare dalle formiche, e se riesco a campare, credi purche che la vita è agra, lassù" (177).

sense of freedom Bianciardi experiences as a traveler in North Africa only reinforces the feeling of exclusion that he endures as a non-northerner in Italy.

As the journey to North Africa draws to a close, the nostalgia of the twenty-day journey and the reality of the return home, and with it the obligations of everyday life, overcome the travelers: "[...] ci sono molti impegni che ci aspettano, su in Italia, e domani ci torniamo, appunto. Già molti impegni. Anzi, troppi impegni ci aspettano in Italia. C'è n'eravamo scordati" (99). Bianciardi, the man allergic to travel, recognizes that these days have been much more than a physical journey through the desert, the oases, the countrysides, and the cities of the Maghreb region. Rather, as we have alluded to above, these twenty days in the midst of strangers and the seemingly unknown have been a rediscovery of the lost world of one's childhood. Having succeeded in stepping outside the boundaries of one's routine and into a world of unrestricted exploration, the travelers are saddened by the reality that there journey is over: "È davvero triste levarsi alle sei, trovare un'alba livida e squallida, oltre che al burino saponaro, in partenza anche lui. Pigliare la strada dell'aeroporto, salutare Marcel Cerdan, salutare Louis Pasteur, salutare un sacco, ormai, di ricordi algerini, infilarsi in un aereo, e sapere che fra un'ora e quaranta minuti sarai in mezzo al traffico romano, via dalla casbah, di cui ti è rimasta la voglia" (103). For Bianciardi, the trip's end is much more than a return to Italy. It represents a return to a condition where man is at the service of objects and machines: "Noi ritorniamo anche nel nostro presente, ritorniamo nella nostra condizione di gente non libera" (99).

WORKS CITED

Angelini, Maria Clotilde. *Luciano Bianciardi*. Florence: Nuova Italia, 1980.

Bianciardi, Luciano. *Daghela Avanti Un Passo!* Milan: Longanesi, 1992.

____. *La vita agra.* 4th ed. Milan: Rizzoli, 1980.

____. *Aprire il fuoco.* Milan: Rizzoli, 1976.

____. *Viaggio in Barberia.* Turin: Edizioni di Torino, 1997.

____. "Lettera da Milano." *Il peripatetico e altre storie.* Milan: Rizzoli, 1976. 220-25.

____. "Libri di viaggio e guide di tutti i tempi." *Le vie d'Italia* LXVII.8 (August 1961): 989-96.

____. "Nasce una nuova lingua." *Playmen* III.6 (June 1969): 8.

____. "E dunque, che lingua fa?" *Notizie letterarie* VI.4 (April 1965): 32-36.

Bianciardi, Luciano, and Carlo Cassola. *I minatori della Maremma*. Bari: Laterza, 1956.

Bianciardi, Luciana, ed. *Carta su carte di ribaltura: Luciano Bianciardi traduttore*. Florence: Giunti, 2000.

Corrias, Pino. *Vita agra di un anarchico: Luciano Bianciardi a Milano*. Milan: Baldini & Castoldi, 1996.

De Pascale, Gaia. *Scrittori in viaggio: Narratori e poeti italiani del Novecento in giro per il mondo*. Turin: Bollati Boringhieri, 2001.

Ferrarotti, Franco, ed. "L'uomo e la macchina nella società." *Terzo Programma* 1 (1963): 256-64.

Leed, Eric. *The Mind of the Traveler. From Gilgamesh to Global Tourism*. New York: Basic Books, 1991.

____. *Shores of Discovery. How Expeditionaries Have Constructed the World*. New York: Basic Books, 1995.

Pasolini, Pier Paolo. "1° febbraio 1975. L'articolo delle lucciole." *Scritti corsari*. Milan: Garzanti, 1990: 128-34.

____. "Diario linguistico." *Dialogo con Pasolini. Scritti 1957-1984*. *Rinascita* 42 (November 1985): 88-104.

Riall, Lucy. *The Italian Risorgimento. State, Society and National Unification*. London: Routledge, 1994.

Vella, Zolita Louise. *Luciano Bianciardi: His Life and His Works. Image of a Dilemma*. Diss. Columbia University, 1976. Ann Arbor: UMI, 1976.

"Gentilissimo Sig. Dottore, questa è la mia vita. Manicomio 1914" La storia di Adalgisa Conti

Daniela Orlandi
DOMINICAN UNIVERSITY

> *"[...] facciamo dunque l'elogio degli uomini illustri, dei nostri antenati secondo le loro generazioni[...]. Di loro alcuni lasciarono un nome...Di altri non sussiste memoria; svanirono come se non fossero esistiti; furono come se non fossero mai stati[...]"*

Ecclesiastico (44, 1.8-9).

In Italia, soprattutto in questo dopoguerra, si è lentamente dato sempre più maggior spazio e voce ai "senza-storia," a quelli di cui "non sussiste memoria," e si è notato come essi avessero cose interessanti e soprattutto importanti da dire, da manifestare. Da anni, vi è così la presenza di questo filone di storici che ha cominciato a occuparsi, dentro o fuori la storia delle classi dirigenti, dei potenti d'ogni fatta e misura. Esisteva ed esiste la classe dei cosiddetti dotti, ed esisteva ed esiste la cultura subalterna e 'alternativa,' che un tempo si esprimeva oralmente e con segni e suoni. Ora sono possibili le testimonianze scritte, in lingua nazionale o/e in dialetti o/e miste. La cultura cosidetta subalterna, dalla quale peraltro tanti valenti scrittori e studiosi hanno attinto, è tale in quanto è stata e continua ad essere priva di potere, compreso appunto quello di esprimersi.

A questo gruppo dei "senza-storia" appartiene il nome di Adalgisa Conti. Adalgisa era una giovane donna di Anghiari ricoverata in manicomio in modo coatto a ventisette anni e mai più uscita fino alla morte, ultranovantenne. Una bella donna, si era sposata tre anni prima del ricovero; a detta di un ex sindaco di Anghiari, era considerata da tutti, intelligente ed estrosa. "Il ricovero coatto in manicomio era avvenuto perchè, secondo una diagnosi medica di allora, era "affetta da delirio di persecuzione con tendenza al suicidio."[1] Nella sua cartella clinica per il periodo

---

[1] Luciano Della Mea in "Prefazione" a A. Conti. *Gentilissimo Sig. Dottore, questa è la mia vita. Manicomio 1914*, p. 12.

compreso tra il ricovero e il marzo 1914 ci sono diverse sue lettere che rivelano, meglio di qualsiasi altro documento, quale delitto sia stato istituzionalmente e culturalmente consumato nella mente e sul corpo di questa donna, "dotata di qualità umane non comuni."[2] Il "delitto" viene scoperto dallo psichiatra Della Mea. Della Mea si trovava tra il 1976 e il 1979 a collaborare con il manicomio di Arezzo[3] e tra i vari compiti compiti che si era assunto c'era anche appunto quello della lettura/studio delle carte cliniche dei lungodegenti, diverse centinaia, per lo più poveri o miserabili, analfabeti o quasi. Fù così che nel 1977 scoprì in una delle cartelle cliniche, fra altre missive, "Gentilissimo Sig. Dottore. Questa è la mia vita" scritta in calligrafia serrata, minuta, sicura da Adalgisa Conti il 25 marzo 1914, cioè a circa quattro mesi dalla sua costrizione in manicomio. Ne la "Prefazione" Della Mea scrive: "Rimasi inpietrito e poi costernato e infine indignato di brutto. [..] Mi rinchiusi, battei a macchina la lettera di Adalgisa, stesi una bozza di progetto editoriale e lavorai [...]."[4]

L'ultima lettera della Conti, che è ragione e sostanza del libro-autobiografia[5] – così come del lavoro teatrale[6] del

---

[2] Ibidem, p. 13.

[3] "[...] Ho pienamente partecipato alla vita interna ed esterna del manicomio di Arezzo, là chiamato dall'amico e compagno Agostino Pirella per il progetto del Consiglio nazionale delle ricerche finalizzato alla prevenzione delle malattie mentali, progetto che avvenne prevalentemente in situazioni di nuova psichiatria detta "democratica" grazie anche all' apporto nuovo dei familiari dei "malati", di enti locali, di sindacati, di scuole, di giornalisti, di diretti interessati provenienti da ogni parte del mondo. Un itinerario difficile, intenso, fecondo dal '68 alla legge 180 inclusa nella riforma sanitaria del 1978" Ibidem, p.11.

[4] Ibidem, p. 12.

[5] Il libro, uscito nel 1978, ha avuto un grande eco di stampa e una buona diffusione in Italia e all'estero.

[6] "Cristina Crippa, attrice che interpreta Adalgisa Conti nello spettacolo spiega l'origine del titolo in "Carissima Adalgisa..." in *Gentilissimo Sig. Dottore*, p. 154: "[...] il titolo "Lola che dilati la camicia" è una canzone, ma una canzone storpiata (dilati sarebbe *di latti*, bianca): è il preludio della *Cavalleria Rusticana*, la serenata di Turiddu a Lola) citata in un racconto di Alda Merini, a cui molto volentieri la rubo, perchè è un verso allegro, ma nella sua alterazione un pò surreale ed esagerato e di colpo tragico."

regista Marco Baliani, *Lola che dilati la camicia*, lavoro basato sull'autobiografia[7] – e che fu indirizzata e consegnata al medico "curante," contiene la storia dei suoi ventisei anni, vissuti per lo più ad Anghiari, fino al momento in cui la disperazione la indusse a prepararsi in casa una morte devota e fiorita.

Parlare oggi di Adalgisa Conti assume più di un significato. "Storie come quella di Adalgisa," così scrive nel 1978 il Collettivo delle operatrici dei Servizi psichiatrici della Provincia di Arezzo, "sono paradigmatiche, perchè mostrano con indiscutibile chiarezza come l'ospedale psichiatrico non è solo un luogo in cui non si cura, ma il luogo dove una persona viene inesorabilmente schiacciata da un apparato teso a ricondurla a uno stereotipo di malato mentale postulato in partenza." Ma nell'autobiografia, che Adalgisa narra con sorprendente sincerità ed abbandono totali, vi è molto di più. Vi è quella che Della Mea definisce "la storia di una sessualità tanto intensa e limpida quanto repressa, che pregiudizi culturali e ignoranza del proprio corpo sacrificano alle esigenze di un marito padrone, quel Probo Palombini del quale Enzo Gradassi, nella sua inchiesta/intervista ad Anghiari, ricostruisce la squallida storia e la tragica fine"[8]; e vi è la storia di rapporti interni a due famiglie piccolo-borghesi -la sua e quella dei suoceri, presso i quali visse durante gli anni di matrimonio- in un ambiente sociale dove la miseria era preponderante.

La storia di sè stessa, raccolta in un libro completato con dati, giudizi, incontri e commenti di chi la conobbe e di chi, a manicomio aperto, l'ha "recuperata" e finalmente curata, non è solo la rievocazione spietata di una vicenda disumana tra le più terribili datata nel nostro tempo, ma è anche e sopratutto, in tutta la sua freschezza anche letteraria, uno strumento di denuncia e di lotta contro le istituzioni segreganti e la violenza del sociale sulle donne. Non è, quindi, solo la storia del 'percorso clinico,' della 'storia clinica' di un "malato di mente" dentro l'istituzione

---

[7] Il testo dello spettacolo teatrale, rappresentato con successo per molto tempo a Milano, è riportato nel libro.
[8] Ibidem, p.14.

manicomiale, ma è anche la storia particolare di una donna, che nonostante abbia un'incredibile coscienza di sè e dei propri bisogni, ed una spiccata capacità di analisi e di autoanalisi, viene, e forse proprio per questo, schiacciata prima dalla violenza del sociale e poi da quella istituzionale.

La particolarità di questa storia, come ripete l'autore, risiede inoltre nella grande capacità di Adalgisa nel 1914 di scrivere di sè stessa con tanta sincerità, penetrazione, capacità di comunicazione e con un così alto grado di coscienza; ingredienti questi, difficilmente associabili a persona internabile in manicomio e che perciò fecero a buon ragione lasciare "impietrito e poi costernato e infine indignato" il Della Mea.

Una donna, inoltre, che per la sua condizione sociale,[9] fu favorita da un livello di cultura non comune a quei tempi. Queste e altre sue peculiarità non fermarono tuttavia la violenza esercitata su di lei per ricondurla allo stereotipo della donna socialmente accettabile, prima, e della malattia istituzionalizzata, poi: il tipo di violenza, cioè, che l'accomuna a tutte le altre donne che hanno vissuto la realtà del manicomio.

Il tema di fondo è quindi, ancora una volta, quello della violenza: quello dell'educazione familiare che per costringere la piccola Adalgisa in un ruolo di "mammina" dei fratelli minori, la "deruba" dei giochi e della spensieratezza dell'infanzia. All'inizio del racconto di sè Adalgisa ripercorre con la memoria quegli anni in cui doveva aiutare la madre maestra, rimasta vedova e con diciotto figli di cui solo otto rimasti in vita: "[...]aiutavo a lavare i piatti, andavo a lavare i panni sudici dei bambini, guardavo i fra-

---

[9] Nell'intervista curata da Enzo Gradassi all'ex sindaco di Anghiari, Antonio Ferrini, rilasciata il 26 ottobre 1977 ad Anghiari, alla domanda di come fosse la condizione economico-sociale della famiglia di Adalgisa e quella del marito Probo rispetto al resto delle famiglie del paese, il sindaco risponde: "Rispetto al resto erano famiglie...agiate. Agiate...di una certa agiatezza...sia per la cultura: la mamma maestra[...]." Ibidem, p. 46. Dell'attività di probo il sindaco ricorda: "Era proprietario della tipografia, qui, Tiberina. Facevano anche un giornale a un certo momento sai? Pubblicavano un bel giornalino che si chiamava, "L'Appennino" che è continuato poi un bel pò. Aveva quattro o cinque tipografi: qualcuno ancora ci è rimasto, qualcuno è emigrato. [...]" (41).

telli, per quanto poca simpatia ci avevo."[10] Il tema della
violenza di una medicina, ignorante da sempre della corporeità delle donne, che la stigmatizza come sessualmente
anormale diagnosticando come "mestruo vicariante" una
emottisi, come si legge dalle "notizie anamnestiche," rile-
vabili dalla sua cartella clinica, compilata dal medico al
suo ingresso in ospedale psichiatrico ("[...]Ha avuto, a dodici anni, una emorragia dalla bocca che fu interpretata
come un mestruo vicariante"); violenza di una cultura che
offre alle donne uno stereotipo rigido a cui conformarsi:
mansuetudine, castità, riservatezza, spacciandolo per
"naturalità," al di fuori del quale c'è solo "devianza," anor-
malità e malattia.

La storia di Adalgisa, storia femminile, è autodenuncia
di una donna "diversa" che ricerca instancabilmente dentro a sè stessa le tappe, le *viae crucis* e le ragioni della sua
diversità. La psichiatria tradizionale, quella in voga soprattutto nei suoi anni, ha pronta la diagnosi: "sindrome
malinconica." In una scrittura fitta, poche pagine senza
letteratura, si autocondanna perchè donna dotata di desideri sessuali. E' del suo sesso di donna che Adalgisa parla, del suo corpo, nell' infanzia e nell'adolescenza, del suo
desiderio limpido e concreto; si assume anche la colpa delle mestruazioni scarse e irregolari che interpretava come
malformazioni organiche attribuendo la causa al fatto che
fin da ragazzina si masturbava:

"[...] Crebbi gracile perchè fui viziosa da masturbare
anche le amiche vicine di casa."[11] Ecco allora che la
masturbazione, nella mente della giovane donna, il piacere
che uno si dà da sè, diventa qualcosa che fa venire addirittura le malformazioni. E' vizioso per la cultura in cui
vive, anormale e quindi, da condannare. Adalgisa parla di
tutto, anche delle più piccole fantasie sessuali, dei desideri
possibili e di quelli che devono rimanere inaccessibili.
Tutt'altro che in preda agli umori del proprio utero e del
proprio apparato genitale, come si voleva farle credere,
Adalgisa sa con precisione cos'è l'orgasmo, il piacere fisico
e dei propri sensi: dichiara di non provare nulla durante il

---

[10] Ibidem, p.19.
[11] Ibidem, p. 19.

rapporto sessuale col marito, assai avaro di attenzioni ed insensibile verso di lei: "freddo, indifferente mai mi baciava con quella voluttà come avrei bramato; e se qualche bacio mi dava, sembrava che me lo desse per compassione o tanto per contentarmi."[12] E continua:

> [...] La notte tornava a ora tarda e io spesse volte non avendo quella soddisfazione che proverebbero due sposi che veramente si amano da me sola provavo strisciando il dito sopra, quel certo non so che mi faceva piacere. Piacere che usando con Probo non avevo provato che una o due volte in tanti anni trascorsi [...] Se Probo mi domandava il risultato, cioè se ero rimasta soddisfatta, sempre dicevo di sì perchè non volevo che mi dicesse: Ma che sei di pietra? Che non senti nulla? Ed io per non arrecargli questo dispiacere che certamente provato soffrivo ma fingevo.

Ma di questo e di altri 'limiti' del marito e della loro relazione, Adalgisa attribuisce a sè soltanto la responsabilità. Probo, che tutti ad Alghieri ricordano come un uomo violento, che frequentava altre donne durante sia il periodo del fidanzamento sia negli anni di matrimonio trascorsi insieme, è nell'autobiografia descritto come "[..] un bel giovane, di carattere d'oro, possidente, e volendo, confronto a lui [lei era] un aborto."

L'uomo che ha firmato la sua sentenza 'all'ergastolo,' ad una vita dietro e sbarre dell'istituzione totale – Adalgisa ha vissuto sessantacinque anni di calvario manicomiale- viene a più riprese giustificato nelle lettere al dottore: "[..] se io non fossi stata di caratteraccio, come mi son sempre mantenuta, non mi avrebbe messo in gattabuia; cioè non volevo dire Sig. Dottore in gattabuia, no, ma a succhiarmi la vita a stilla a stilla, finchè a lui piacerà. Del resto con Santa rassegnazione sopporterò, lotterò, finchè vorrà il destino, Probo, e i dottori.[...]"[13] E qualche pagina più avanti:

> [...] Solo le dico che con Probo non ci siamo mai presi di carattere: eravamo troppo differenti uno dall'altro; lui troppo

---

[12] Ibidem, p. 28.
[13] Ibidem, p. 23-24.

buono e io troppo cattiva, perciò ha fatto bene come ha fatto,
anzi troppo bene al momento mi tiene, poichè meriterei con
tutto ciò che ho fatto, esser messa in una grotta come fece
Santa Margherita di Cortona espiando i peccati commessi,
soffrendo fame e freddo, in un posto lontano dal consorzio
umano[..][14]

Sempre autocondanna, colpevolizzarsi, mai accusa o ran-
core verso di lui che sposò dopo tante traversità e come
scrive: "nel tempo delle pubblicazioni fatte all'insaputa
delle nostre famiglie e del Paese; perchè amoreggiava con
altra ragazza chiamata Vittoria [..]."
Adalgisa, pur non volendo ferire il marito, reclama
tuttavia il suo diritto al piacere e, senza alcun disprezzo,
anzi con molta pietà,ogni volta che ne parla, sente di non
voler condividere il destino di quelle donne "che passano
la vita come schiave del marito" o "fatte vecchie, attem-
pate, zitellone," perchè "tradite, abbandonate" da un qualche uomo. Ma ha su di sè il peso di una terribile aggra-
vante: è una donna sterile, le sue richieste sessuali che
non servono alla gratificazione dell'uomo-marito e non
sono legittimizzate dalla sofferenza del parto e dai sacrifici
della maternità, sono allora pretesa ingiustificata, un "ca-
priccio" come lei le definisce spesso, una lussuria inac-
cettabile per una donna "normale." E Adalgisa con il suo
"caratteraccio," comincia a sbattere la testa contro i muri,
i suoi tentativi di riscatto e riaffermazione non riescono
più a convincere la sua mente stanca; comincia a dubitare
del valore delle sue parole, della sua innocenza e della
propria normalità.
Adalgisa, come detto più addietro, vive però anche in
una condizione incredibile, insieme di assoluto privilegio[15]

---

[14] Ibidem, p. 30-31.
[15] "Nell'ospedale psichiatrico tradizionale non era consentito possedere
nulla, neanche una penna, appunto; qualunque oggetto può costituire
uno strumento da usare a scopo aggressivo o autolesivo in nome di
quella "pericolosità" che, secondo l'ideologia psichiatrica su cui è
modellata la pratica manicomiale, è caratteristica del malato mentale.
Per molti anni i ricoverati hanno continuato a denunciare in Assemblea
generale come una delle pratiche più violente e umilianti la "fruga" e cioè
la perquisizione sistematica a cui venivano sottoposti in certe ore della

e di violenza: può scrivere, quindi è "alfabeta," anche se scrive la propria storia sempre vigilata da un'infermiera. La scrittura è qui allo stesso tempo possibilità di salvezza e di condanna. Aver accesso alla scrittura e scrivere significa distinguersi rispetto alle altre pazienti, di comunicare come in un 'gioco' di cui comunque non conosce le regole, e si chiede se l'aver confessato i suoi desideri più intimi sia stato un bene o un male. Si veda ad esempio quando scrive: "[...] non so se scrivere tutte quelle sudicionerie ho fatto bene o male." Il gioco è infatti nelle mani del'uomo, il Dottore, è lui a cui la scrittura è destinata, e lei vuole uscire. Il Dottore diventa inoltre il solo luogo di una seduzione altrimenti impossibile al corpo femminile, che in un ospedale psichiatrico ha già subito la negazione della sessualità. Scrivere diventa l'arte della seduzione della donna.

Ma Adalgisa vuole anche uscire dal manicomio, e conosce un solo modo per rapportarsi a quel "Dio" maschio che è il dottore: la seduzione. Scrivere diventa il tentativo di seduzione tra vittima e carnefice: "[...] mi mandi pure per serva, bambinaia, coca, o sguattera; perchè lei per me è un Dio; e pur volendo tutto può."[16]

Si è detto prima, scrittura come privilegio. Ne il "Dibattito" che si è svolto tra coloro che lavorarono in manicomio negli anni in cui Adalgisa fu rinchiusa si legge:

Jozzia:[17] "[...] Ma forse non era soltanto un fatto di ceto sociale ma anche di cultura: un'altra degente non era in grado di dire niente, di scrivere niente, e invece l'Adalgisa era in grado di scrivere, di parlare, d'interessare insomma. In sintesi, la sua appartenenza a un ceto sociale più elevato rispetto alla massa dei ricoverati dell'ospedale e l'avere una certa cultura ha stimolato moltissimo il medico a occuparsi di lei al punto tale che, secondo me, lei è molto migliorata. Noi sappiamo che tante volte il semplice fatto d'interessarsi di una persona, di occuparsi di lei, di parlarci, è già terapia. [...]"

giornata per controllare che non si fossero impossessati di un qualsiasi oggetto [...], op.cit., nota n.5, p. 80.
[16] Ibidem, p. 31.
[17] Piero Jozzia, il medico del reparto dove Adalgisa era ricoverata negli ultimi anni della sua vita.

Dal diario clinico del medico curante abbiamo prova infatti del suo miglioramento, eppure nulla è stato fatto per farla uscire; e più il tempo trascorreva e più il suo stato mentale cominciava a deteriorarsi: *"Guidelli*[18] 'Ma poi c'è stato un rifiuto da parte della famiglia, e lei si è abbondonata completamente.'

Jozzia: 'Ma perchè a quel punto non è continuato l'interesse di coloro che la curavano? Probabilmente perchè lei era diventata come le altre e dal quel momento, infatti, nella sua cartella non c'è alcuna differenza dalle altre cartelle del manicomio' *Giorgeschi*[19]: 'Finito l'interessamento dei suoi, finito quello dei medici, lei si è ritrovata abbandonata da tutti ed è rimasta qui dentro.'

La storia di Adalgisa, della donna che è "rimasta dentro," è una storia che non può non colpire. Essa avrebbe potuto rimanere comunque una delle tante storie di donne "impazzite" e rinchiuse, storie che, negli ultimi anni soprattutto, giornali, romanzi, cartelle cliniche, inchieste e la nostra stessa quotidiana esperienza ci hanno consegnato, vite in molti modi tanto simili alle nostre ma che ad un tratto svoltano nell'afasia, nella distruzione, nella violenza, nel delirio. Un sogno nero da cui è difficile svegliarsi.

A ridare il volto e la familiarità di tratti ad Adalgisa ridotta ormai alla pura corporeità, non bastano evidentemente le informazioni a cui i cronisti tentano di dare un' immagine plausibile all'orrore e alla violenza. Qualcuno, un giorno, ha scritto che il giornale è un'ubriacatura di fatti atroci che accompagna la colazione dell'uomo civilizzato e che come l'ubriacatura passa senza lasciare traccia.

Invece, per Adalgisa anche se molto tardi, è accaduto un evento forte e imprevisto che muta la nostra possibilità di rapporto con la sua vicenda: a Luciano Della Mea viene chiesto, nel 1977, "un intervento storico-politico-sanitario" che desse un giudizio, situandolo storicamente, sui criteri

---

[18] Franca Guidelli ha fatto 15 anni di servizio nel reparto di Adalgisa Conti.

[19] Margherita Giorgeschi, 14 anni di servizio.

scientifici in base ai quali lei venne internata [...] nel Manicomio di Arezzo"[20]
Con la pubblicazione del libro il Della Mea non ha voluto fare "una perizia che davanti ad un tribunale immaginario assolvesse la Conti con formula piena e suonasse condanna senza appello per il manicomio e la psichiatria del suo tempo, esecutori materiali di un delitto su commissione di una marito violento e di una società repressiva e sessuofobica come l'Italia giolittiana dell'inizio del secolo." Non c'è assoluzione o condanna con la pubblicazione dell'autobiografia della Conti. All'apparire della 'vita vera' di Adalgisa, l' "estraneità' dei perbenisti si incrina e la 'vita vera' dell'autobiografia conferma ulteriormente e con forte evidenza quanto la donna, soprattutto, in Italia sia stata oggetto di una grande violenza psichiatrica che ha cercato di imporle il silenzio.

Dopo sessantacinque anni, attraverso l'autobiografia, Adalgisa Conti riesce invece finalmente a parlare, a imporre all'istituzione e al mondo il suo punto di vista, il suo sistema di valori, la sua cultura, cioè la storia della sua vita e della sua "malattia," vista da se stessa e non da un medico e dalla sua cartella medica. La sua autobiografia ci insegna che dietro un volto scavato c'è una storia, spesso disperata, talvolta di lotta contro un destino miserabile di violenza e di segregazione. Grazie allo smantellamento del manicomio fianco a fianco con gli internati la psichiatria ha iniziato ad intravedere una rivendicazione dietro un delirio, una domanda di libertà dietro un gesto di rottura o ribellione, e ad accettare che dietro un 'vissuto di colpa' vi è spesso la protesta contro una violenza sociale ripetutamente subita.

---

[20] Da "Appendice 2. L'Interpretazione negate," in *Gentilissimo Sig. Dottore questa è la mia vita*, p. 72.

INDEX

Aaron, Daniel, vi
Adler, Alfred, 59,
Ahmad, Aijaz, v-viii
Angelini, Maria Clotilde, 130
Annali d'Italianistica, ii, iii

Bataille, Georges, 49
Benhabib, Seyla, 23
Benjamin, Jessica, 82, 85, 87
Benjamin, Walter, 5
Bertolucci, Attilio, 17, 18
Bertolucci, Bernardo, 74-88
Bianciardi, Luciano, 118-32
Bianciardi, Luciano, and Carlo Cassola, 125
Blum, Cinzia Sartini, 23
Bondanella, Peter, 76
Bongie, Chris, 2, 3, 5
Brunetta, G.P, 51, 52
Butler, Judith, 38

Calvino, Italo, 7-8, 12, 14, 20-1
Camaiti Hostert, Anna, i
Camboni, Marina, 15-6, 18, 23
Celati, Gianni, 1-14
Challis, Chris, 37
Chiavola Birnbaum, Lucia, ii
Clifford, James, vii
Clover, Carol, 38-9
Cohan, Steven, 53, 54, 55, 56
Connors, Robert and Cheryl Glenn, 90
Corrias, Pino, 127
Creed, Barbara, 38-9, 45-6
Crippa, Cristina, 134
Croce, Benedetto, 1
cultural studies, i-viii

Dalle Vacche, Angela, 1
De Lauretis, Teresa, 88
De Pascale, Gaia, 3-5, 26, 123
De Rosa, Tina, 98, 102, 104, 113-5
Della Mea, Luciano, 133, 134, 135, 136, 141
demonization of women, 62-5
diaspora, i
Dombroski, Robert, ii
dominant cultural studies, iii-iv
Duggan, Christopher, and Christopher Wagstaff, 52, 53

Ehrenreich, Barbara, 55, 56
Ellwood, D.W. and G.P. Brunetta, 51
experiential cultural studies, iii-iv

Ferrarotti, Franco, 120
Ferrini, Antonio, 136
Ferroni, Giulio, 1-2
Fisher, Jack, 88
Fiske, John, iii
Fiumi, Cesare, 29-37
Fontaine, Andre, 56

Gambino, Richard, 95
gender, i, vi, 21, 43, 53-7, 62, 65, 74-88, 133-42.
Ginzburg, Carlo, 7
Giorgeschi, Margherita, 141
Gnisci, Armando, iii
Gradassi, Enzo, 135, 136
Guidelli, Franca, 140
Gundle, Stephen, 51
Gunew, Sneja, viii

Index

Index

White, Hayden, 25
Whyte, William J. Jr., 54
Wilson, Sloan, 73
Wylie, Philip, 56

Zavarzadeh, Mas'ud, iii-v,
   viii

FRED MISURELLA
Lies to Live by
Vol. 38, Stories, $15.00

STEVEN BELLUSCIO
Constructing a Bibliography
Vol. 37

ANTHONY JULIAN TAMBURRI, ED.
Italian Cultural Studies 2002
Vol. 36, Essays, $18.00

BEA TUSIANI
con amore
Vol. 35, Memoir, $19.00

FLAVIA BRIZIO-SKOV, ED.
Reconstructing Societies in the Aftermath of War
Vol. 34, History/Cultural Stud., $30.00

A.J. TAMBURRI, M.S. RUTHENBERG,
G. PARATI, AND B. LAWTON, EDS.
Italian Cultural Studies 2001
Vol. 33, Essays, $18.00

ELIZABETH GIOVANNA MESSINA, ED.
In Our Own Voices
Vol. 32, Ital. Amer. Studies, $25.00

STANISLAO G. PUGLIESE
Desperate Inscriptions
Vol. 31, History, $12.00

ANNA CAMAITI HOSTERT &
ANTHONY JULIAN TAMBURRI, EDS.
Screening Ethnicity
Vol. 30, Ital. Amer. Culture, $25.00

G. PARATI & B. LAWTON, EDS.
Italian Cultural Studies
Vol. 29, Essays, $18.00

HELEN BAROLINI
More Italian Hours & Other Stories
Vol. 28, Fiction, $16.00

FRANCO NASI, A CURA DI
Intorno alla Via Emilia
Vol. 27, Culture, $16.00

ARTHUR L. CLEMENTS
The Book of Madness and Love
Vol. 26, Poetry, $10.00

JOHN CASEY, ET. AL
Imagining Humanity
Immagini dell'umanità
Vol. 25, Interdisciplinary Studies, $18.00

ROBERT LIMA
Sardinia • Sardegna
Vol. 24, Poetry, $10.00

DANIELA GIOSEFFI
Going On
Vol. 23, Poetry, $10.00

ROSS TALARICO
The Journey Home
Vol. 22, Poetry, $12.00

EMANUEL DI PASQUALE
The Silver Lake Love Poems
Vol. 21, Poetry, $7.00

JOSEPH TUSIANI
Ethnicity
Vol. 20, Selected Poetry, $12.00

JENNIFER LAGIER
Second Class Citizen
Vol. 19, Poetry, $8.00

FELIX STEFANILE
The Country of Absence
Vol. 18, Poetry, $9.00

Published by BORDIGHERA, INC., an independently owned not-for-profit scholarly organization that has no legal affiliation to the University of Central Florida, Florida Atlantic University, or State University of New York—Stony Brook.

This book was set
for Bordighera Press by
Deborah Starewich
of Lafayette IN, U.S.A.

www.ingramcontent.com/pod-product-compliance
Lightning Source LLC
Chambersburg PA
CBHW021157010426
R18062100001B/R180621PG41931CBX00011B/17